# THE VALUE OF
# THE DIAMOND

# THE VALUE OF THE DIAMOND
## A Jim Caldwell Story

### Book 3

# Keith H. Adkins

ISBN-13: 9798985856989
Printed in the United States of America
ChrisJen Publications
www.keithhadkins.com
Cover design by: ebooklaunch.com

# Contents

# ACT IV
## THE PRISON LIFE

# The Value of the Diamond

## PROLOGUE
### Life after Death

It was a rather chilly Sunday morning in the Phoenician desert. As the sun was peeking over the McDowell Mountains, Big Nose Kate was desperately trying to wake up. She had made a commitment to a daily journey to the gravesite of Jim Caldwell, yet a couple of days later it was the last thing she wanted to do. Her grief weighed her down so much she could barely move. She just couldn't get that image out of her head of Jim's body hanging from a rope. Kate thought that maybe she could dull the pain with alcohol, after all, it always worked in the past. That frightening memory jolted her awake.

She sat up and slowly rubbed her eyes, trying to find focus, then clumsily got dressed in bed. Kate stepped over some of the Hole in the Rock Gang sleeping on the floor of the boarding house, and headed for the door. The morning sun was streaming through the window as she walked by, then she opened the door, locked it behind her, and left. The direct sunlight made everything feel warmer, as she began her trudge to the abandoned diamond mine that served as Jim's tomb. "Why am I doing this?" Kate asked herself, but the truth was that she just wanted to be near the man she loved more than anything. It seemed like an endless journey as she dragged one leg in front of the other, while aching all over.

When she finally arrived, she noticed something strange about the stone that covered the entrance. Looking closer, Kate was surprised to see six of the seven seals broken. Dmitri, the Russian overlord for Phoenix, had ordered his soldiers to spread melted wax between the stone and mine entrance. He also told them to press his ring into the wax to make an official insignia. This was to provide proof that nobody could tamper with the dead body, because Marshal Garfias heard some wild stories about resurrecting from the dead. Out of fear, the soldiers decided to seal the tomb seven times for extra protection.

Kate could see that the first six seals were broken, so she blinked her eyes and moved in closer. The remaining seal was definitely missing the insignia, and she guessed that the soldiers were simply in a hurry, causing them to miss putting the final insignia in place. Out of curiosity, she reached her hand toward the seventh seal, and it too broke. Now a lot of folklore develops around unusual stories like these, but what people later said was that, "there was silence in heaven for about half an hour."

What happened next took Kate's breath away, and she became paralyzed with fear. While standing at the entrance, the gigantic boulder slowly rolled to the side. Her instinct was to run, but her feet wouldn't move. Right then a wonderful fragrance wafted out, and the spices that were left around Jim's body helped bring Kate's mind back to the moment. "What should I do?" she wondered, as the cool air also drifted out of the diamond mine and further helped to clear her mind.

Against her better judgment, and almost like an out-of-body experience, she slowly stepped into the cold, dark, makeshift tomb. Once inside, her eyes took a bit of time to adjust, so she rubbed them, and was stunned because she couldn't believe what she saw. It was something that would forever be talked about in the annals of time. To her absolute terror and deep confusion, she was confronted with...are you ready for this?...

nothing. As in no body. As in an empty tomb that had been meticulously sealed to prevent this sort of thing from happening. At that point she nearly fell down trying to get out of there, because one's rationality is completely lost in moments like that.

Once out of the mine, she fled in terror, wondering if the grave robbers were still nearby. Then she remembered that the tomb was still sealed, which further confused her. After fumbling to unlock the door at the boarding house, Kate breathlessly burst through the door. The boys were awake and Pedro said, "Whoa, there! What's your problem? And for heaven's sake, lock the door." For a moment she thought that the nothingness she saw in the diamond mine was a cue to say nothing...so she didn't...then she did. She mumbled some confusing gibberish which brought the rest of the gang together to see what was going on.

"Take a deep breath," said Pedro, so Kate complied because she was already feeling a bit light-headed. Johnny had just finished making a pot of coffee, so he handed her a cup of Arbuckles' Ariosa Blend.

Kate said thanks and took a few sips, then they sat and waited to hear what was going on. She rocked back and forth trying to soothe herself, and finally screamed, "Jim's body's gone!" and, as you can imagine, the reaction was varied.

Jimbo said, "Not surprised they broke in and stole his body. The marshal wanted that to happen, 'cause of all that talk 'bout Jim risin' from the dead."

Johnny mumbled, "Maybe she's back to drinking."

Then Pedro said, matter-of-factly, "Just tell us what happened."

Kate took a moment to compose herself, and with a bit of tremble in her voice, said, "When I got to the tomb this morning, the stone was still blocking the entrance."

"So how'd ya know his body was stolen?" asked Matt.

"Just let her tell her story," growled Bart.

After a moment Kate explained, "Six of the seals were broken, but the seventh seal was still in place."

"So his body wasn't stolen?" asked Carly.

"I don't know," replied Kate, with a bit of exasperation. "All I know is that I reached toward that seventh seal and then it broke."

"So you broke it?" inquired Junior.

"No!" yelled an irritated Kate. "But then the boulder rolled to the side." Now they were getting interested.

"What did you find?" asked an impatient Pedro.

"Nothing" said Kate. "The tomb was empty."

"Either the tomb was empty because the stone was moved before you got there," suggested Johnny, "or it was moving because you were tipsy." Several laughed, but the look they got from Kate quickly ended their fun.

"This ain't no laughing matter!" complained Kate.

Then Pedro said, "Okay, I'll go see for myself what's going on." He left in a bit of a huff, and went to the outskirts of town where the mine was located. While approaching, he thought to himself, "If Jim got out of that tomb, when it was still sealed and he was dead, the ole worthless diamond mine just might find it has value."

It was full daylight when he arrived, and he was beyond surprised to see the stone rolled away. He thought it was too big and heavy for Kate to have moved it, so he started feeling fear as he stooped to look in. All he saw was the Indian blanket Jim's body had been draped in, and lots of spices strewn about, still filling the air with a wonderful aroma. One would think Jim's

# The Value of the Diamond

body was stolen, but not Pedro. He decided to believe Kate about the breaking of the seventh seal, and being the first one into the formerly sealed tomb. What Pedro decided to believe was about resurrection. People had talked about it since Ezekiel's prophecy in chapter 37, which said, "You shall know that I am the LORD, when I open your graves, and bring you up from your graves, O my people. I will put my spirit within you, and you shall live." (vv. 13-14).

Pedro was beside himself with excitement. He went running back to the boarding house and yelled gleefully, "I knew it! If anyone could beat death, it was gonna be Jim." Others kind of wanted to go see, but since two had already shared the same story from separate trips that the tomb was empty, they decided to stay. That night, the Gang closed and locked their boarding house room, out of fear that they would be blamed for taking Jim's body. Was Kate right, that the body was taken, or Pedro, that Jim had resurrected from the dead? Tommie didn't particularly care, so he went out to have a drink at a bar. Several rushed to the door to lock it after Tommie left, because whatever the truth was, strange things were certainly happening.

It turned out that Tommie missed the most momentous occasion one could possibly imagine. As the Gang sat around the table and chairs in the lamp-lit room, Jim himself appeared to them. To say the least, they were in shock as they rubbed their eyes. Pedro was the first to speak, saying, "Locked doors couldn't keep him out any more than a closed tomb could keep him in." The darkness of the room caused the others to squint, because they feared they were seeing a ghost. Then Jim spoke, "Peace be with you." He told them that the good words he had shared with them on the hillside, the parables he told, and the great powers God wrought through him, were now theirs to continue. They were speechless, and then frustratingly, Jim disappeared.

Pretty soon there was a knock on the door, and they all nearly fainted. Pedro sheepishly made his way to the door and asked in a befuddled manner, "Who's there?" The answer quickly came back, "It's me, Tommie. Who'd ya think it was?" A relieved round of laughter broke out and Pedro unlocked the door and let him in. Jimbo told Tommie the story about Jim's appearance, and Tommie was the only one who laughed. "I thought I was the one who had too much to drink," retorted Tommie, and this time nobody laughed. He looked around, saw folded arms and serious looking eyes, and said "I'm sticking to my guns on this one. You don't call me Doubting Tommie for nothing!"

About a week passed and the Gang was confused, because they didn't know what to do. They stayed put all week in the locked room and things were started to get musty. They believed that Jim had been resurrected from the dead, and they really felt it was important to be of one accord, but Tommie wouldn't budge. They routinely gathered at the dinner table during that week, and talked about what Jim had said. It would be easy enough to continue sharing his stories and parables, but they weren't too sure they understood what Jim meant by God's powers now being theirs to continue. Unfortunately, they also rather taunted Tommie about his unbelief, and he was beginning to feel excluded. That's when Jim appeared again in the boarding house.

The Gang was overjoyed to see him, but Tommie was the one this time who was speechless. They all moved in closer to be near Jim, while Tommie moved back. He hit the bunkbed behind him and fell onto the bottom mattress. Everyone looked back, and Tommie appeared as white as the ghost he thought he was seeing. Jim looked at him and said, "Tommie, stand up." He knew he was in trouble, but not sure why. As he stood up, nearly knocking over a lantern, Jim said, "Do not doubt, but believe." Tommie gathered his senses and delightfully surprised everyone by saying…"I believe!" Jim then said, "Blessed are those who will never be able to see me, but choose to believe." Jim then once again disappeared, and Tommie took some time to be embarrassed.

It was a rather sleepless night for all of them, as they pondered the meaning of everything that had happened. The next morning they discussed what to call themselves, because they felt 'Hole in the Rock Gang' was about the past. Since Pedro was the go-to guy for naming, they asked him for some ideas. After scratching his head a bit, he mentioned that when Jim appeared, he called them to continue the things he had done. A huge grin then spread across Pedro's face and he said, "I guess you could say we were 'called well.' Get it? Let's call ourselves Caldwellians." Nobody liked it at first, but somehow the idea stuck, and after a while they adopted their new name.

———————

Meanwhile, before continuing with other things that happened after Jim's resurrection, we need to first get caught up on a couple of important events from the fall of 1881. Deputy U.S. Marshal Virgil Earp moved from Prescott to Tombstone, to help deal with the outlaw Clanton Gang. Virgil quickly appointed his brother, Wyatt Earp as the acting City Marshal, who was also pleased to see his good friend Doc Holliday had arrived in town. On October 25, Ike Clanton was openly breathing threats against the Earps and Holliday. After a heated argument, the unarmed senior Clanton member said "Get ready for a showdown!" The next day the Clanton Gang met in a vacant lot to bushwhack Doc Holliday, but they were surprised when the Earps showed up with Doc. The Clanton Gang made their way toward the O.K. Corral, and as the Earps passed by, they found the troublemakers waiting at the end of an alley. Virgil tried to arrest them, but what happened next was a blur. Some of the Clanton Gang cocked their pistols, shots were fired, and several died. The Earps and Doc Holliday were tried for murder, but it was decided that they acted within the law.

Another important thing that happened in the fall of 1881, was the end of the Russian Invasion. Back in the motherland, Tsar Alexander II was assassinated. His successor was his son, Alexander III, who wanted to avoid his father's fate. The first thing he did was to reverse the liberal reforms of his father by assuming autocratic rule. This kind of oppressive rule needed the full force of his military, so he recalled his troops from southwest America. They moved out about as fast as they moved in, and the invasion that started without bloodshed, mercifully ended in a withdrawal without bloodshed.

---

In the meantime, the boarding house they were staying at was starting to smell, and Pedro was feeling a bit antsy. "I don't like it," announced Pedro, "that we're now just a group of eleven, after Bennie hung himself."

# The Value of the Diamond

"Let me remind you that Bennie's death made us a group of twelve," countered Big Nose Kate.

"Not really," complained Pedro. "You liked to call us a baker's dozen, but we ain't thirteen any more either."

"Right," argued Kate, "because we're now a group of twelve!"

"But the twelve," continued Pedro, with frustration in his voice, "referred to the twelve men, and now Bennie is gone."

"Men!" Kate stomped her foot on the ground and raised her voice, "At least Jim didn't discriminate against women!" Most of the men in the room looked uncomfortable, but didn't want to deal with her.

"So, what's yer point, Pedro?" asked Bart, proving that Kate was right about men, and even more correct about Jim.

"We need to honor Jim's plan of having twelve of us," explained Pedro.

Carly then chimed in with, "We've got enough problems. Don't need more, unless ya gots a solution."

"Not that hard," said Pedro, "all we have to do is add another to our group."

"Since you don't seem to want to follow Jim, when it comes to equality," offered Kate, "I guess I need to push you all on this issue, so I vote that you add me." The guys rolled their eyes and ignored her, which made her even madder. "So, at least we can all agree on one thing. You guys, and I do mean guys, find it difficult to live the life Jim taught!"

"You're right," Pedro said in a dismissive way, then suggested "let's add one of the people among the crowds who heard Jim talk and saw the great things he had done."

"You mean one of the men among the crowds," complained Kate.

Talking as if Kate wasn't even there, Johnny asked, "How about Clint?"

Almost at the same time, Bart said "I was impressed with Cooper.

Pedro then suggested, "Let's do this the way Jim did things. Let's pause in prayer and ask for guidance from God."

Kate threw her arms up in the air and said, "Nice job of practicing selective spirituality."

They agreed that they were doing a nice job, and continued to ignore her because now she was using big words that they didn't understand. Then they bowed their heads, including Kate, who was now outside their prayer circle, because they wanted Kate to understand that they were going to do things the way Jim did. Pedro simply prayed "Our father in heaven, please show us which one of the two people you have chosen."

Kate added, "Lord, he means, which one of the two men, because Pedro really isn't interested in you having your way, if it includes a woman." Now she was stepping on toes, as if she were a preacher. Come to think of it, she was the first person ever to preach the good news of the empty tomb. This comment rather abruptly ended the prayer, without so much as an "amen."

At least Matt affirmed the hypocrisy as he complained, "This was easier when Jim was around."

"I agree," said Pedro with a lot of frustration, "but this is what we have now. Anyone have an idea which person God wants us to choose?"

"No," answered Jimbo, "but I've got a coin. How about I flip it? If its heads we go with Clint, and if its tails we go with Cooper.

"And if it lands on its edge, we go with me," Kate suggested sarcastically. "And what a great idea  to let God speak through gambling!"

The men agreed that God was speaking through Jimbo, not Kate. Then Pedro angrily offered out of his biblical ignorance, "God surely couldn't speak through a donkey." Several nodded in agreement, so he flipped the coin. All eyes were steadfastly watching the coin as it went into the air. It came down, hit the floor awkwardly, and rolled toward the wall. They almost knocked each other over following it, and their eyes went wide open as it started to tip against the wall.

Pedro stomped the floor in anger and the coin fell over. He happily said, "Tails. Looks like God wants Cooper to join us."

"Looks more like Pedro wants another man to join us, if you ask me," complained Kate as she turned and walked away.

Nobody was asking Kate, and since Bart was the one who suggested Cooper, he was sent out to retrieve him. The room was rather chilly that hot afternoon in the Arizona desert, so they sat and waited without talking.

Cooper was downtown working at the new post office when Bart found him, and Bart simply said "Cooper, the Lord has chosen you to become a witness with us to Jim's resurrection." This became the first sign that things were going right, because Cooper was happy to be added to the group. When Bart and Cooper returned to the boarding house, they were very excited and began sharing the stories of Jim's resurrection and his appearances.

"I guess I just have one question," mentioned Cooper. "I heard a lot of his stories and saw many of the things he did. How did Jim do all those things?"

"It was the power of God working through him," stated Pedro, as a matter-of-fact. "And when the resurrected Jim appeared to us right here in this room, he said that the stories and powers were now ours to continue."

"I guess I have another question," announced Cooper. "If you have so much power, why are you all holed up here like a bunch of scared kittens in a box?"

"Good question," stated Johnny.

Bart seemed embarrassed for a moment, and decided they needed to be empowered by their personal stories, so he shared how his life had changed. Matt gave a glowing testimony of the radical change in his lifestyle, and Kate had the most impressive story of the effect Jim had on her life. Cooper decided right then and there that he was dedicating his life to becoming what they were starting to call Caldwellians.

Rather on a high, Pedro said "Let's go to The Rusty Tavern. I sense something great is getting ready to happen," and the others could feel it, too.

As they opened the door to leave, Kate said, "Kinda feels like we're leaving the tomb. Maybe now we can start living the resurrection life."

They all agreed, but Pedro cautiously said, "Or at least we'll try."

Getting in the last word, Kate said, "Nope. This new life is something we do or don't do. No such thing as trying. That would be like being a little pregnant!"

# ACT I
## THE ROAD TO TUCSON

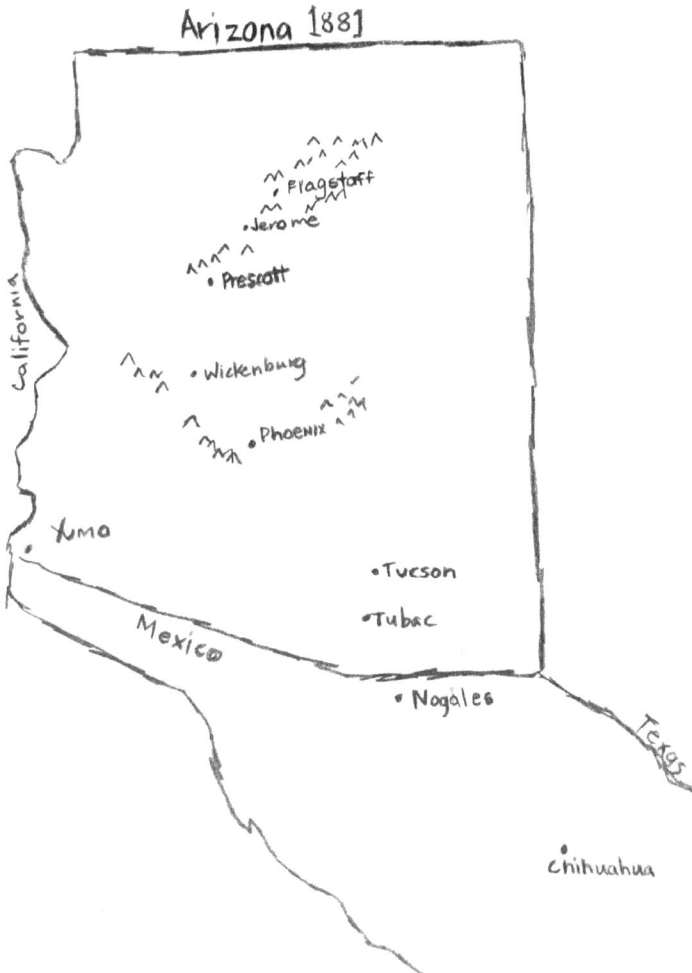

Arizona 1881

## SCENE ONE
### The Caldwellians

I t was exactly fifty days since the Jewish celebration of Passover, making this the Jewish day of Pentecost. This day commemorates the power of God coming down to Mount Sinai, giving the gift of the Torah. Nobody in the group knew that because there weren't many Jews in the Arizona Territory. After the relatively short ride to The Rusty Tavern, they were surprised to see a large crowd gathered inside and out. Our Caldwellians dismounted and headed through the multitude. As they expected, there were no seats or tables available in the Tavern, but soon Jimbo announced that a table was freeing up outside. They packed themselves around the table with the late morning sun glistening on their faces.

Suddenly there was a loud sound like a pack of coyotes, followed by what looked like sparks of fire resting on the heads of each of the Caldwellians. Pedro looked over and saw fire even resting on the head of Kate, and she returned a peaceful smile. At that point hey were filled with the Holy Spirit and began speaking in other languages, which amazed and astonished the onlookers. One man said, "That guy is speaking Apache," and another said, "I hear someone speaking Russian. I thought we were rid of them!" A large group of Chinese immigrants had come for the California Gold Rush, and a Chinese man who had settled in Phoenix announced that he heard someone speaking Chinese. All were amazed and perplexed and more than curious. Finally, a man came stumbling out of the Tavern and said "I know drunk talk when I hear it!"

Pedro then stepped forward and got everyone's attention.

# The Value of the Diamond

He wasn't sure what to say, but he knew Jim's spirit would be with him, so he opened his mouth and spoke from the heart. "I assure ya we ain't drunk. We just arrived and couldn't even find a table, much less place an order, but listen to what I have to say." He paused for a moment, surprised to see people paying attention, then said, "Jim Caldwell, as you well know, performed deeds of power, wonders, and signs that God did through him. Then you had a fake trial, and sentenced him to be hung by the Russians."

"Rightly so," yelled a large man holding a mug of beer.

Ignoring him, Pedro continued. "But God raised him from death, and freed him from the diamond mine that served as his tomb, because death could not hold him. Jim was raised up to heaven by God, and all thirteen of us here today are witnesses." He again flashed a smile at Kate and she returned an approving look.

Someone yelled, "That's a bunch of hogwash!" and went back into the tavern. Others went back to eating and drinking, while still others came forward and asked what they should do.

Pedro said to those interested, "Change your lives, and be baptized, so that your sins may be forgiven; and you will receive the gift of the Holy Spirit."

So those who welcomed his message were baptized that day. They headed to the nearby Agua Fria River, where Pedro, Jimbo, and Johnny just naturally waded out. The rest of the original Caldwellians lined people up to get baptized, and they were overwhelmed to see more and more people coming down from the Rusty Tavern. It was an exciting and heart-warming time, as God smiled on them. Someone yelled, "Look, a rainbow around the sun!" It became a fitting end to a memorable day, as people left, filled with the Holy Spirit.

# The Value of the Diamond

An ever-growing number of Caldwellians began devoting themselves to the teaching of Jim, as taught through the original Caldwellians. They began gathering daily for fellowship, and prayer, and learning. Many exciting things started happening over the next several weeks, and people were in awe because wonders and signs were being done by the Caldwellian leadership.

Soon they settled into the Catholic Church in downtown Phoenix, now that the Russians were gone, and the priest was happy to let them use it for their new movement of the Holy Spirit. They also did a rather strange thing, probably to show their commitment. The followers sold everything they had, then the leaders distributed the proceeds to all, as any had need. Things were going very well indeed for the Caldwellians, and their numbers continued to grow.

One day Pedro was at the Church for some prayer time, when a man who hadn't walked since birth was carried to the entrance. The man hadn't been to the church for a long time, due to the Russians, and was happy to be back in his favorite begging spot. When Pedro was done, he headed to the exit, and the lame man asked him for money. Pedro looked intently at him and said, "I got no money." The man looked away in frustration, then Pedro said, "But what I have I give you; in the name of Jim Caldwell, stand up and walk." The man felt his ankles strengthen, then Pedro took him by the hand and helped him stand up. He then ran around the street in from of the church praising God.

People came pouring into the church, because they knew the man, and were amazed when they heard what Pedro had done. They hailed Pedro as a hero, brought him back into the church, and said they wanted to hear more from him. The priest was there, and offered to let Pedro speak from the pulpit. Pedro stepped up and said, "Jim Caldwell did many great works, and he always said it was the power of God working through him. When he was resurrected from the dead, we saw him, and he told us that the powers were now ours to continue. To this we are witnesses. And the lame man now healed is a testimony of God's power, to all of us gathered here. Change yer ways, and turn to God so that your sins may be wiped out."

While Pedro was speaking, Marshal Garfias was just outside the church and had several people complaining to him. The marshal headed into the church with several of his deputies, interrupted Pedro, and declared, "People are annoyed." He then said, "You can't be claiming that Jim was resurrected from the dead." He then explained, "I didn't care for that Russian Dmitri, but he had a great idea about sealing Jim's tomb. That way we would know his body hadn't been stolen. Fact is, the seals were broken, so it's not too complicated to understand how his body disappeared. You yourself probably took it!" The crowd started yelling at the marshal, so he drew his gun and shot it into the air to squelch any questions about his authority. He then arrested Pedro, who was still at the pulpit, and put him in custody. One might think that would stop this new group, but many more became believers that day.

The next day, the clergy showed up at the jail and asked Pedro, "By what power did you heal that man?"

Then Pedro, filled with the Holy Spirit, said to them, "If you are questioning me because of a good deed done to someone who couldn't walk, and are asking how he was healed, let it be known to all of you, that he was healed in the name of Jim

# The Value of the Diamond

Caldwell, whom you hung and whom God raised from the dead."

Having nothing to say in opposition, the clergy retreated just outside the jail for a discussion. They said, "What will we do with him? Everybody already knows what he did. Let's join the marshal in warning him not to speak about Jim." So they returned to the jail and ordered him to be silent about Jim Caldwell.

Pedro then shocked them with his response, "Whether it is right in God's sight to listen to you rather than to God, you must judge. As for me, my answer is 'No!' I will not keep from speaking about all that I have seen and heard."

After the marshal released Pedro, he went back and told all of the believers what the clergy had questioned him about. In return, they prayed for boldness to continue the signs and wonders through the name of Jim Caldwell. After the prayer, something like an earthquake happened, and they were all filled with the Holy Spirit. They found that they were of one heart and soul and agreed to speak with boldness. With great power the Caldwellians went about giving their testimony to the resurrection of Jim, and they were filled with grace. They continued to care for one another's needs through the proceeds from selling their property.

But a man named Jesse, with the consent of his wife Sadie, sold a piece of their property. Then they decided to keep back some of the proceeds before laying it at Pedro's feet. Normally, this would not be a problem, but Pedro's spiritual authority was at stake. As is common in a small community, everyone knew everyone else's business, and soon this minor problem came to Pedro's attention. Pedro knew that the community decision to give property was not required, it was simply voluntary. Being caught between his authority and their choice, he decided to spend some time in prayer.

God nudged Pedro's mind toward a story in 1 Kings 14:1-8, so Pedro opened a Bible and read the story. It troubled him deeply, because he didn't get the point. He read it several times, and soon wished that Jim was there to help him. All of a sudden he realized it was about deceit, and the evil it brings. Pedro thanked Jim in his heart, called Jesse to himself, and asked, "Why has evil filled your heart to lie to the Holy Spirit and to keep back part of the proceeds of the land?" Not only did Jesse refuse to answer, but many of the disciples were listening. Pedro then asked, "How is it that you have contrived this deed in your heart?" Again, there was no answer. Then Pedro declared with powerful authority, "You did not lie to us but to God!" Immediately Jesse got on his horse to flee, but he only got a few feet away until his horse stumbled. Jesse fell off his horse, landed on his head, broke his neck, and died. Those who witnessed this thought it might be a good idea to be honest.

About three hours later, word got around about what happened to Jesse. Crowds started gathering, as is so common when terrible events occur. Then Jesse's wife Sadie returned from a short visit with a friend. She didn't know what happened to her husband, and nobody wanted to talk about it. Pedro heard she was back, so he called for her, and said, "Tell me whether you and your husband sold your land." Sadie said with a bit of confusion, "You know we did." The crowd made a muffled sound, then Pedro said, "Why did you put the Spirit of the Lord to the test?" Now she was very uncomfortable and started to sweat. She looked around and saw everyone watching her, so she rather angrily stammered, "I don't know what you mean." Pedro clearly explained that the common life they all were in was first and foremost about responding to the nudging of the Holy Spirit. He then said, "When evil fills the heart, there is no room for the Holy Spirit." Immediately, Sadie clutched her chest, fell down at his feet and died. Yet again, there was fear about what it meant to be committed to this group of believers, between deaths and healings.

Word got around about this second death, and the original Caldwellians found themselves rather isolated. At the same time, stories were also spreading about the many signs and wonders that were happening. The leaders gathered each day at the Catholic Church in downtown Phoenix, where nobody dared to join them, but the people still held them in high regard. Actually, the number of believers kept growing, mainly due to the healings the disciples were performing. People showed up each day while the Caldwellians continued the work of Jim Caldwell. Maybe the most interesting thing of all was that people were starting to gather from towns around Phoenix; from Prescott and Tucson and Tombstone. They even saw people from Wickenburg and Vulture City, and they were all cured of various infirmities.

Just as things seemed to be going well, the clergy became jealous. They easily convinced Marshal Garfias to put the Caldwellian leadership in jail, where the most unexpected thing happened. During the night, an angel appeared and said to them, "Go back to the church and tell the people the whole message about living the Caldwellian life." As Pedro was about to mention they were locked in jail, the door swung open. Pedro, Jimbo, and Johnny looked at each other then stepped out. They looked around and since they saw no guards in sight, they shrugged their shoulders and left with smiles on their faces.

While the disciples were obeying their divine calling the

# The Value of the Diamond

next morning, the clergy showed up at the jail. They found the jail empty, rubbed their heads, and wondered what might be going on. Then someone from town burst through the front door of the jail and said, "The men you had arrested yesterday are in your church, and they're back at it, teaching the people!"

The church's priest led the posse back to his church, went in and said to the disciples, "We gave you strict orders not to teach in the name of Jim Caldwell." Pedro answered, "Yeah, and you had us arrested, but you can see how well that worked out." The priest was fuming as Pedro said, "We must obey God rather than any human authority." When the clergy heard this, they were all enraged and wanted to kill Pedro, but a deputy showed up and talked the clergy into thinking rather than feeling.

The deputy took them to a back room of the church where the priest angrily said, "This is my church. Pedro's the problem." The deputy said, "Calm down. Even the marshal doesn't know what to do with them. But let's try this. Leave them alone, and if what they do and say is of human origin, it will fail; but if it is of God, you will not be able to overthrow them." This reasoning convinced the clergy, but on their way out, leaving the Caldwellians in, the priest yelled back with his fist raised, "Do not speak again of Jim Caldwell!" As the clergy passed through the door, Pedro looked back at his disciples and said, "This ain't over, fellas."

Now during those days, when the disciples were increasing in number, a problem came to Pedro's attention. Their idea of meeting the needs of all wasn't working, so Pedro called the whole community together and said, "We are growing fast, and that's a good thing, but needs are going unmet. We've gotta continue Jim's works and words, but I think some need to be appointed to distribute our communal possessions." There was an audible sigh of relief because quite a few had been discussing the problem, and they were more than ready to hear a solution.

Pedro continued, "Let's get seven people of good standing. People who are full of the Spirit and of wisdom, to appoint to this task. That will give the rest of us plenty of time for prayer and sharing our stories with others." This pleased the community of believers, and the first name they came up with was Jack. He was a man full of faith and the Holy Spirit. The other six who were appointed were Rose, Boone, Carter, Hank, Belle, and Cheyenne. This group of men and women were brought before the Twelve, who laid their hands on them and offered prayers for their work.

They created a system to manage the assistance to those in need, and as new people joined, they gave the group their possessions. Hank and Belle were in charge of selling the items. Cheyenne and Carter were responsible for the money. Then Rose, Boone, and Jack took care of distributing the money as people had need. Great things continued to happen around Phoenix and even many of the clergy joined the movement.

Jack became the man of the hour. He did his work making sure the community's possessions were meeting the needs of all, and in his spare time he did great wonders and signs among the people. He was a likable sort, and people enjoyed him. Well, not all of the people. Some tried to argue with Jack, about who was in the most need. It seems that even when you are about doing good things in the name of the Lord, someone will find fault, but they could not withstand the wisdom and the Spirit with which he spoke.

# The Value of the Diamond

Not quick to back down, the trouble makers started a rumor that Jack spoke blasphemously against God. This would not be tolerated, so the clergy had him dragged before them. As Jack stood up, they expected to see an angry face, but instead they saw that his face was like that of an angel.

The priest of the Catholic Church, where the twelve had begun their movement, asked him straight out, "Have you been blaspheming God?" Jack replied with a testimony from his heart: "The God of glory appeared to our ancestor Aapo, and said 'Leave your country and your relatives and go to the land that I will show you.'"

"Yah, why don't you leave?" yelled one of the clergy.

"Let him speak," responded another.

"Aapo left his country of Guatemala," continued Jack "and settled at Calakmul. After his father died, God had him move from there to a land of promise."

"Yah, not like this God-forsaken place!" yelled someone in the growing crowd of listeners, as several laughed.

Jack continued, "Then Aapo became the father of Hugo, and Hugo became the father of Tobillo, and Tobillo became the father of the twelve patriarchs."

"We know our Bible!" complained one of the clergy, angrily.

Jack ignored him and said, "The patriarchs sold Eloy into Honduras, but God rescued him and enabled him to win favor with the King, who appointed him ruler over Honduras. Now there was a famine, and our ancestors could find no food. But when Tobillo heard there was food in Honduras, he sent our ancestors there on their first visit. On the second visit Eloy made himself known to his brothers, and Eloy's family became known to the King. Then Eloy sent and invited his father Tobillo to come to Honduras. He died there as well as our ancestors, and they were laid in a tomb."

"I don't hear any blaspheming going on here. I say let Jack go," suggested one of the clergy who had recently joined the movement.

"I want to continue," offered Jack, "because the story gets better. At this time Abund was born. For three months he was brought up in his father's house, but then he was abandoned. The King's daughter adopted him and brought him up as her own son. So Abund was instructed in all the wisdom of the Hondurans and was powerful in his words and deeds.

"When he turned forty, it came into his heart to visit his relatives. When he saw one of them being wronged, he killed the Honduran."

"Now we're talking," a cowboy in the crowd said with a smile. "Sounds like our Wild West." This time others hushed him, because they liked hearing a good story.

Again Jack continued, "The next day he came to some of them as they were quarreling and said 'Men, you are brothers; why do you wrong each other?' But one pushed Abund aside, saying, 'Who made you ruler and a judge over us? Do you want to kill me as you killed the Honduran?'" An uneasy feeling went through the crowd at this point, as murder seemed to be brewing in their attitudes. "This cast great fear into the heart of Abund and he fled. He became a resident alien in the land of San Salvador and became the father of two sons."

"You might be thinking about packing your bags yourself, there young man" said another cowboy. Then he ominously said, "We don't cotton to no blasphemers."

"Forty years later," Jack went on, seemingly unaware of the growing anger in the crowd, "an angel appeared to him in the flame of a burning bush. When Abund saw it, he was amazed.

# The Value of the Diamond

As he approached, there came the voice of the Lord: 'I am the God of your ancestors, the God of Abund, Hugo, and Tobillo.' Then the Lord said to him, 'Take off the sandals from your feet, for the place where you stand is holy ground. I have heard the groaning of my people in Honduras and have come down to rescue them. And now I will send you to Honduras.'

"Doesn't that sound like blasphemy?" inquired a person in the crowd.

"No," said the priest. "At least not yet."

Then Jack said, "It was this Abund who led his people out of Honduras. He performed many wonders and signs in Honduras, at Lake Izabal, and in the wilderness for forty years. Our ancestors were unwilling to obey him, and wished to return to Honduras. They told Abund's brother, 'Make gods for us who will lead the way for us.' So they made a calf, offered a sacrifice to the idol, and were delighted with what they had done."

"Is this guy supporting idolatry?" quizzed a clergyman who wanted to get rid of Jack.

"Let him talk," said the priest. "I think the way he's telling this story is giving us plenty of rope to hang him."

"Our ancestors," Jack said with growing strength, "had the tent of testimony in the wilderness. Then they brought it with Geovanni to Tenochtitlan, and it was there until the time of King Montezuma. But it was the Spanish conquistadors who built God's temple, so hear me out. The Most High does not dwell in houses made with human hands. As the prophet Isaiah says,

> 'Heaven is my throne,
> and the earth is my footstool.
> What kind of house will you build for
> me, says the Lord,

or what is the place of my rest?
Did not my hand make all these
    things?'"

Anger was at an all-time high now in the crowd, but Jack expressed it first and directed it at them. "You stiff-necked people, uncircumcised in heart and ears, you are forever opposing the Holy Spirit, just as your ancestors used to do. Which of the prophets did your ancestors not persecute? They killed those who foretold the coming of Jim Caldwell, and now you have become his betrayers and murderers. You are the ones that received the law as ordained by angels, and yet have not kept it!"

In hindsight, Jack would have been better off keeping his temper, because the clergy certainly didn't. They became enraged, were grinding their teeth, and wanted blood. That's when Jack was filled with the Holy Spirit and gazed into heaven. There he saw the glory of God and Jim Caldwell standing next to him. "Look," Jack said, "I see the heavens opened and Jim Caldwell standing next to God!"

That was it. The clergy were beyond furious, then rushed in on Jack. They knocked him down, dragged him out of town and prepared to hang him. While they tied the noose around Jack's neck, he prayed, "Lord, receive my spirit." As they kicked the support out from under Jack's feet, he was heard saying "Lord, do not hold this sin against them." When he had said this, his body swung slowly as his last breath left him. Someone in the background looked on with a rather evil smirk of approval. That someone was Jose Maria Perez, who hated a fake story more than anything.

The next day a severe persecution began against the

movement started by Jim Caldwell, and it was Jose Maria Perez who rallied the oppression. He made a visit to Marshal Garfias and got deputized, so he could track down Jim's followers and arrest them. So Jose Maria Perez began his legal campaign of hatred and violence. He entered house after house and asked if they were followers of Jim. If they said "no" he would leave them alone, but for those who confessed their allegiance to the Caldwellians, he dragged them off to the downtown jail and the marshal gladly locked them up.

---

After the tragic loss of Jack, Rose stepped up to the task of sharing the stories of Jim Caldwell. She was one of the seven, along with Jack, who had been appointed to dole out the proceeds to those in need. After the persecutions began, and the followers were scattered, Rose went down to Tucson. She spoke with great eloquence about Jim and the crowds listened eagerly. She was rather short of stature, so she stood on a wooden crate, and they were astounded at the signs she did. She exorcised demons out of many who were possessed, and cured many others who were paralyzed or lame. So there was great joy in that city.

In contrast to Rose, there was a magician named Alexander Herrman. He had traveled all over the world, and now was settled into Tucson and performing his art. He was well known as the first magician to pull a live rabbit out of a hat, and the people of Tucson were amazed by him. They would often say, "This man is the power of God that is called Great." That created a tension in the town about who they thought was the greatest, so they listened carefully to what Rose was saying. It didn't take long until many realized that Rose was promoting God, and Alexander was promoting himself.

When those who believed Rose was the real thing, because she was proclaiming the kingdom of God in the name of Jim Caldwell, they were baptized. At first, Alexander was jealous. He wanted the crowds for himself, so he paid attention to what Rose had to say. He had been more attracted to Rose's spectacular accomplishments than her spiritual message, but actually, he simply found her quite enticing. His travels made it difficult to think about marriage, but now he was settled down. He didn't think he would have any chance with Rose, because he was a bit short and stout, so he did what he could do. Alexander became a believer and was baptized. Truth is, what he started dreaming about was to tour with Rose for profit, and of course, to marry her.

Now when the Twelve up in Phoenix heard that Tucson had accepted the word of God, Pedro and Johnny went down to pray for them. They soon discovered that the people were only baptized, but had not yet received the Holy Spirit. Then Pedro and Johnny laid their hands on them, and they received the Holy Spirit. This was a profound moment in the life of the believers, as they praised God, exchanged hugs, and offered holy kisses. Now when Alexander saw this great event, he offered money, saying, "Give me also this power so that anyone on whom I lay my hands may receive the Holy Spirit." But Pedro said, "May your silver perish with you, because you thought you could obtain God's gift with money! You have no part or share in this, for your heart is not right before God. Repent, and pray to the Lord that you may be forgiven."

Alexander was stunned, and said, "Pray for me that I will

not lose my silver." Pedro shook his head in frustration. He couldn't believe how lost Alexander was, especially considering he had been baptized. Pedro called Rose over and had a long chat with her about the difference between baptism by water and baptism by the Holy Spirit. He said, "Baptism by water remembers what Jim received from his cousin the Dipper, and baptism by the Holy Spirit is the leading of Jim here and now. After a good discussion, because this was new to all of them, Pedro and Johnny got on their horses and returned to Phoenix.

After they left, an angel of the Lord said to Rose, "Get up and ride your horse toward the south to the road that goes down from Phoenix to Chihuahua, Mexico." (This is a wilderness road.) So she got up and went. Now there was a court official of the President of Mexico, who was in charge of his treasury. He had come to Phoenix to worship and was returning home. When his stage coach stopped at Nogales for more passengers, he pulled out his Bible and started reading from the prophet Isaiah. Then the Spirit said to Rose, who had also stopped for a break at Nogales, "Go over to the man on the stage coach who is reading his Bible." So Rose went and heard him reading the prophet Isaiah. Rose asked, "Do you understand what you are reading?" He said "How can I, unless someone guides me?" Fortunately, for Rose, this man was bilingual, so the conversation was quite easy. Now the passage he was reading was this:

> "Like a sheep he was led to the
> slaughter,
> and like a lamb silent before
> its shearer,
> so he does not open his mouth.

# The Value of the Diamond

In his humiliation justice was denied
him.
Who can describe his generation?
For his life is taken away from the
earth."


Now the court official asked Rose, "About whom, may I ask you, does the prophet say this, about himself or about someone else?" Then Rose began to speak, and starting with this scripture, she proclaimed the good news about Jim Caldwell. Since there was a pond at the stagecoach stop, the official asked to be baptized. Rose was very pleased and the stagecoach driver said, "Okay, but you need to hurry. I don't like to have my passengers wait too long." So they waded into the pond, and Rose baptized him in the name of Jim Caldwell.

---

Meanwhile, Jose Maria Perez had no idea he was preparing for a life-changing event. The family surname was of biblical origin and it meant "breach." It comes from Genesis 38:27-29: "When the time of her delivery came, there were twins in her womb. While she was in labor, one put out a hand; and the midwife took and bound on his hand a crimson thread, saying, 'This one came out first.' But just then he drew back his hand, and out came his brother; and she said, 'What a breach you have made for yourself!' That story provided the origins for the family name of Perez."

Jose felt there was destiny and identity in his last name.

# The Value of the Diamond

Since breach means breaking or failing to observe a law, he decided early in his life that he would leave family when he turned eighteen. It was an unspoken law that family was everything, and the daughters were expected to stay and help with raising the family. And if there was one thing his mother said more than anything else as he was growing up, it was, "People can cause trouble about a whole lot of things, but don't dare cause trouble for my family." And Jose knew that leaving would be difficult for the family, so it would be no easy decision.

Jose was a Mexican American who was born in 1862 in San Jose, California, and his family worked the fields for a living. They picked peaches, pears, apricots, and plums, and Jose himself starting working at the age of five. That's when the beautiful valley, with its ideal weather, produced bumper crops of the fruits, which also created a problem. The glut of fruit sent the prices plummeting, which gave rise to the need for preservation. Drying and canning solved the problem, but Jose's father decided to switch his career to carpentry.

Throughout the 1870's, young Jose worked beside his father, learning every aspect of the trade. He became an apprentice to his father, and learned how to make baseboards, stairs, and doors. He also learned the art of framing a building with a saw, chisel, and plane. It was during this time that Jose had an accident with one of his tools that would affect him the rest of his life. He never would share details, but he referred to the incident as his 'thorn in the flesh.' Although he was raised in a good Catholic home, Jose became bitter toward religion. He had prayed for healing from his 'thorn in the flesh,' and when that didn't happen, he lost his faith. He also pledged to fight any religious folk who got in his way.

Meanwhile, Jose was going to stick to his plan to leave

when he turned 18, so he started listening for opportunities as that age approached. Sure enough, in 1880, he heard about a tent city starting to grow in Jerome, Arizona. A copper mining claim was made just four years before that, in 1876 by Al Sieber, but his claim didn't arouse much interest. When word finally got around in 1880 that there was a lot of copper in the Black Hills of Arizona, hopes were high and the young Jose was ready to leave. He saddled up a horse and left family, in pursuit of a dream to use his carpentry skills in an exciting environment. As he rode off, he looked back and saw his mother fold her arms and turn her back to him.

He arrived in the late summer of 1880 and was deeply disappointed. The town was precariously anchored on the steep slope of Mingus Mountain. The trip up the mountain was almost roadless, and the young Jose passed hard-looking prospectors and miners with horses, mules, and burros. While the copper mining continued to look promising, he simply was too early. He made cabinets for buildings that were getting started, but he was itching for more. He also heard the winters could be difficult in the mountain town, so he rethought what to do. Hearing that a little town called Phoenix down in the Arizona desert was already growing, he left in the early fall.

When he got to Phoenix, he heard strange stories about a man named Jim Caldwell who healed people, and then was supposedly resurrected when he died. If Jose hated one thing more than religious lies, it was the "thorn in his flesh." He lived with pain constantly and wished he could get healed, and also realized that his first few months out on his own were not going well. The one thing he felt good about so far was leaving Jerome. He figured there was no way that little town in the mountains would ever successfully produce copper mines.

# The Value of the Diamond

That's when he came across the hanging of the disciple named Jack. He indeed smirked about this event, because he didn't believe for one minute all this talk about healing and resurrection. He reasoned to himself, "If healing could take place, don't you think Jack could have used some help right then and there? And if resurrection is true, I trust we'll be seeing a lot of Jack around town." He sneered again, just remembering the story. From that point on, all he wanted to do was go around persecuting anyone who called themselves Caldwellians. As mentioned earlier, he even got Marshal Garfias to give him the right to drag believers to jail.

Jose had found his new calling. He hated the disciples of Jim so much, that he asked Marshal Garfias if he could look for disciples in other towns. The marshal said that he had heard about things happening down in Tucson, so Jose received a letter giving him permission, that if he found any of these fake news folks, he could have them bound, arrested, and brought back to Phoenix. The marshal then got a couple of deputies to accompany Jose, because he was growing weary of the tall tales people were sharing about Jim escaping the diamond mine after he died. This would also solidify his role of being in charge, now that the Russians were gone.

As Jose was approaching Tucson, he was stopped in his tracks. A violent dust storm bore down on them, and all he could think about was a story from his Catholic upbringing. He remembered that "the heavens were opened" and the prophet Ezekiel saw "a great cloud with brightness around it" (chapter 1, verses 1 and 4). But that was just a story, Jose thought, and this was real, so what could he make of it all?

As he was struggling forward through the sand and dust, Jose tripped over a rock and stumbled to the ground. He

# The Value of the Diamond

thought he heard one of the deputies talking, so he asked "What?" Instead of hearing one of them, he heard a voice from heaven asking, "Jose, why do you persecute me?"

Jose asked, "Who is it?"

A reply came back that shocked his soul, "I'm Jim Caldwell."

Jose replied, "But I don't see anyone."

The voice continued, "That's because I died and have been resurrected to heaven. But get up and go on in to Tucson, and you will be told what you are to do."

The deputies were getting concerned along about this time. The dust storm passed quickly, but Jose was standing again and they saw Jose talking to thin air. They thought maybe he bumped his head when he stumbled over a rock, so one of the deputies asked, "You okay, Jose?" Jose stood up and looked around, and couldn't find the deputies. "We're right here!" said one of them. Jose rubbed his eyes for a minute, then looked again.

"Jose, can you see?" asked the other deputy.

"No!" yelled an angry Jose, "I've probably just got sand in my eyes."

Then the heavenly voice returned, saying, "Have the deputies help you, because you will be blind for three days."

Jose wasn't sure what to say to the deputies. He was still trying to grasp the enormity of what just happened. He knew that it must be true, because Jim said something about persecution, and that was indeed what he was doing to Jim's followers. All of a sudden he felt like his gut had just been punched. He bent over in pain from the realization that he had been dead wrong, and then fainted.

The deputies helped him back to his feet when he woke

up and said, "Come on, we don't have far to go." That gave Jose some peace of mind, because Jim said he would find out more when he got there.

Now there was a disciple in Tucson named Remington, whom Rose converted. God said to him in a vision, "Remington."

He answered, "Here I am."

God said to him, "Get up and go to the street called Calle Real, and at the house of Arlo, look for a man of Jerome named Jose. He has seen a vision of you laying your hands on him so that he can see again." Now Remington wasn't very fond of this task, because he had heard of all the evil Jose had done in Phoenix. But the Lord said to him, "Go, because I have chosen him to bring my name before the people of the Arizona Territory." So Remington obeyed. When he arrived, he was a bit surprised to find it was all true, then he announced that the Lord had called him to this task. When Jose confirmed about the vision, Remington laid his hands on Jose's eyes and something like rattlesnake scales fell from his eyes. Everyone was in shock because Jose could see again. The deputies left at that point because things were getting a bit too strange for them.

Jose then jumped up and ran around the house like a kid with a new toy. He said that God told him he needed to get baptized, so Remington took Jose to where Rose was staying. The wondrous story delighted Rose, so they went to Sabino Creek. Rose explained that water baptism was done because it is what Jim Caldwell had done, but cautioned that he also needed the baptism of the Holy Spirit. Soon they were wading into the water and Jose was baptized. To Rose's surprise, Jose came up out of the water, and began praising God. Jose was such an entirely new man, that Rose suggested he even change his name. From that day forward Jose decided to be known as Pablo.

For several days, Pablo remained with the Caldwellians in Tucson. When asked by anyone who came by, why Jim Caldwell was so important, he taught them that "Jim became the Son of God by resurrection from the dead." All who heard him were amazed at the incredible change in his life, because he was previously known as the persecutor of Caldwellians. Well, not all were amazed. Some Catholics were enraged that this fake story about Jim Caldwell wasn't going away, so a small, malevolent group, plotted to kill him. Fortunately, some of Pablo's fellow believers heard about the deadly plot against their new found friend, and they informed him of the problem, and helped him get out of town under the cover of night.

When Pablo arrived in Phoenix, he tried to join the believers. They were having nothing to do with him, because they didn't believe for one minute he was now a disciple. But a woman named Daisy took him to the twelve, because she knew Big Nose Kate would help. Once Pablo gained audience, he told about his road to Tucson experience. They listened intently and soon were overjoyed about this great news. Well, not everyone. Pedro had spent so much time with Jim while he was alive, he felt his lengthy experience with Jim was far more important than a brief encounter with the risen Lord. After all, the original twelve had that kind of experience, too. Even Tommie.

So why were people finding something special about Pablo's experience on that road? Pedro couldn't quite put his finger on what bothered him, but he sensed it had something to do with authority. It just wasn't right that some trouble maker would come into their midst, then claim to be a changed person and be immediately accepted as important. Pedro was fuming inside, but pretty soon had an idea. "I think," announced Pedro, "that Pablo should go back where he came from, er, I mean to Jerome." So Pablo agreed to defer to Pedro's leadership, and headed to Jerome to teach the small but growing town about Jim Caldwell.

Since Pedro was feeling threatened by the new upstart Pablo, he felt it would be a good time to continue the works of God. After all, Jim had said it was their job, not Pablo's, so he went about looking for someone who needed the power of God in their life. Soon enough he came across a man who had been bedridden for eight years, because he was paralyzed. Pedro walked right up to him and said, "In the name of Jim Caldwell, and through the power of God, be healed!" And immediately the man got up, and walked, and many that day turned to the Lord. This new movement of the Holy Spirit brought comfort to the followers and they grew in numbers.

Now in Tubac there was a disciple whose name was Grace. She was devoted to good works and acts of charity, and was well loved in her little town. Suddenly she became ill and died. Her friends wrapped Grace's body in a shroud, leaving her head uncovered for the undertaker to finish caring for her properly. Unfortunately, the undertaker had been called down to Tombstone to help with the many bodies of cowboys who were being killed in gun fights. Tombstone was trying to move past the infamy of the OK Corral, but it was still the wickedest city in the Old West. While there, the Undertaker taught some locals how to embalm, because folks were being preserved in barrels of whiskey until they could be properly buried.

Since Tubac was near Tucson, the Caldwellians there

heard about Grace's death, and immediately sent word asking for Pedro's presence. Pedro saw this as a continuing sign of his God-given power. He knew he could use it as long as it was clear that it was the power of God, not his own. When Pedro arrived, Grace's friends took him to an upstairs room. The women were crying and showing Pedro some of the things Grace had made. Pedro then asked them to leave, and he knelt down and prayed. While praying, Pedro felt God's power filling him, and he said, "In the name of Jim Caldwell, and through the power of God, be healed." Pedro could hardly believe he had just said that to a dead body, but sure enough, Grace opened her eyes. He then realized why he needed the women to leave, because they would surely have fainted, and some may even have fallen down the stairs.

Grace appeared scared when she saw Pedro. "Are you a ghost?" asked Grace. Pedro laughed and replied, "Look who's talking!" as he pointed at her clothing. She looked down and saw that she was wrapped in a death shroud and became confused. "Am I in heaven?" asked Grace. Pedro quickly said, "No," which frightened her even more, then introduced himself and explained that God had just brought her back to life. He then called the women and other believers who had gathered there, to come back up. When they saw Grace lying in her death bed, with a death shroud on and her eyes open, yep, several women fainted. Others told Pedro to go back downstairs so they could get her properly dressed. As you can imagine, this became known throughout Tubac and Tucson, and many more became believers in the Lord.

# The Value of the Diamond

## SCENE TWO
### Nogales and Chihuahua

Many things were happening in the 1880's in the Arizona Territory. Stagecoach service was popping up here and there by independent companies, making travel easier. One hindrance occurred in 1884, when Wells Fargo kept getting robbed on the way out of Vulture City, and decided to suspend service. John Butterfield saw an opportunity, and added passenger service to his mail routes. He was awarded a large contract from the US government to establish mail service from St. Louis to San Francisco. The trip took 25 days and traversed southern Arizona. The problem here was that it took four days and 27 stops just to cross Arizona, from Texas to California.

Another important development that effected the spread of the good news for believers, was the end of the Apache Wars in 1886. Starting in 1849, during the Mexican-American War, this series of battles was the longest war in US history. The last major battle ended with the surrender of Geronimo. The Army used over 5,000 men to finally wear down Geronimo and his band, and secure his defeat at Skeleton Canyon in Arizona. The 65-year-old war chief was taken to Florida and imprisoned for two years. In the meantime, their children were sent to Pennsylvania to learn English and the American lifestyle.

The biggest event occurred on July 4, 1887, with the arrival of the Southern Pacific train in Phoenix. Since neither the Gila River nor the Salt River flowed enough for ships, it wasn't easy to transport building materials to the growing town located in the middle of the desert. The advent of rail service triggered rapid growth in Phoenix, complemented by the fact that land could be purchased cheap. Business was booming, the population was growing, and the time was ripe for evangelism.

---

First, the disciples agreed that they were cowboys, and would pursue their task on horseback as much as possible. Trains and stagecoaches were fine, but they never wanted to have to wait on others to do their work. Meanwhile, Pedro and Pablo continued to struggle over power. Pedro had certainly established himself as the front runner of Jim's command to continue God's works through him, but Pablo had a fascinating story about Jim in heaven. A decision was made to form a church council (what could go wrong with that?) to decide how to handle the work of spreading the word about Jim Caldwell.

The current twelve, plus Kate, sent word to Pablo up in Jerome to gather with them at the Rusty Tavern for this important task. The next day, after Pablo arrived, there was excitement in the air. Pedro, Jimbo, and Johnny seemed like naturals to offer leadership to the meeting, since Jim had especially chosen them to be with him at important moments. So, of course, Pedro started the meeting.

"How do we split up duties?" asked Pedro.

"Bart, Matt, and I," suggested Phil, "could share the good news to the people of Prescott and Agua Fria Valley since we're from there." Everyone agreed.

"Andrés, Jimbo, Johnny, and I," offered Pedro, "should probably stay in the Phoenix area since it's starting to grow."

# The Value of the Diamond

Again, there was no dissension. Tommie, Junior, and Thad decided to go to Tucson, and Carly, Cooper, and Kate chose Tombstone.

"That was easy," announced Pedro, "so I think we're done." As people started to stand up, Kate noticed Pablo sitting in the corner with his arms crossed.

"Didn't we forget someone?" asked Kate. This was followed by an awkward silence until Pedro frowned and said, "What are we to do with him, anyway?"

Nobody had a suggestion, so Pablo mentioned that even though he was raised in California, he was raised bilingual. "I think I'd like to take the word to Mexico."

"Sounds great to me!" said Pedro sarcastically.

"Likewise!" said Pablo, as he seethed about the obvious disrespect Pedro showed him in front of the group. At that moment, Pablo wished we wasn't a Caldwellian. He imagined for a delicious moment knocking Pedro down and dragging him to jail. But that's not who he was now. At least not who God wanted him to be. Pablo discovered that keeping the old pre-Jim Caldwell life at bay was going to be very challenging.

Then everyone left.

---

Pablo stayed that night at a small hotel next to the Rusty Tavern. He was deep in prayer when he sensed God calling him to a new village on the border between America and Mexico. That little boundary place became a part of the United States in 1853, following the Gadsden Purchase, and it became very interesting in 1880. It seems that a couple of Russians by the names of Isaac and Jacob Isaacson, decided to homestead a trading post on the site. People accepted them because they said they would defect as soon as the Russian Invasion was over, and sure enough they did. As the Russians departed, nobody noticed the two who stayed way down on the southern side of the Arizona Territory. The town was initially named Isaacson, but in 1883 it was renamed Nogales, referring to the large stand of walnut trees that once stood nearby.

Pablo gathered some supplies and headed off for a God-directed adventure. As he rode through Phoenix, he saw Kate standing outside the boarding house. She told him that she was leaving the next day with Carly and Cooper to evangelize Tombstone, so if he waited they could ride together. It sounded like a good idea to get to know them better, so he happily stopped and stayed with them. Pablo and Kate had a lot of useful connections, so they had a great talk.

"How do you deal with rejection?" queried Pablo, fresh off the frustrating meeting at the Rusty Tavern.

"You're talking about Pedro, aren't you?' clarified Kate.

Pablo said, "Sure. Who does he think he is, anyway?"

"Well," responded Kate, "in answer to your first question, I deal with rejection by focusing on the joy of knowing Jim. For the second one, Pedro obviously thinks he's the boss. I've had my share of frustrations with him."

"So how do you focus on Jim?" asked Pablo.

"Sometimes it's difficult," explained Kate. "The shame I feel about my old life can be overwhelming."

Pedro agreed by saying, "I used to hate religion. But then I was struck down on the road to Tucson by the risen Jim, and I'll never be the same. By the way, Kate, I was surprised when you decided to evangelize in Tombstone. Wouldn't that place be full

# The Value of the Diamond

of temptation for you?"

When Carly and Cooper nodded in agreement, Kate asked, "So what should I do? I already agreed with Pedro's plan to split up the duties."

They all four laughed and Carly said, "Sounds like a new plan would be best. Why don't you go with Pablo?" This time they all four agreed, then went to bed and got some sleep. Pablo slept best, being filled with the thought of usurping Pedro's authority. The next morning they got on their horses and began their journey. Passing Superstition Mountain, they settled in for a long ride to Tucson. That's where they parted ways. Pablo and Kate needed to go due south to Nogales, while Carly and Cooper were heading southeast for Tombstone.

After saying their goodbyes, Pablo and Kate traveled first to Tubac. Nestled between the Tumacacori and Santa Rita mountain ranges, Tubac was established in 1752 as a Spanish Presidio. Pablo rather enjoyed the small village, so they stopped to water their horses at the Santa Cruz River and visit with some locals. It was a beautiful area, with cattle drinking water by the sandy banks. He enjoyed a few good stories, but being from San Jose, California, Pablo was mostly fascinated to find the connection between Tubac and San Francisco.

It turned out that in 1777, his own hometown was founded as Pueblo de San José de Guadalupe, the first city founded in the Californias. Just two years earlier, in 1775, an expedition led by Lieutenant Colonel Juan Bautista de Anza marched through Tubac, on their way to settle Alta California. It was a grueling 1,200-mile journey through the desert, into California, and up the coast. Traveling with 240 people and 1,000 head of livestock, they made their way up to the bay area and founded the Presidio of San Francisco in 1776.

# The Value of the Diamond

Knowing they were on a missional journey to Mexico, the two left Tubac sooner than they wanted. He could see the mining areas that stopped during the Civil War that the locals told him about. He was also told that the fighting wasn't against confederate soldiers, but against Apaches. A shiver went down his spine as he continued his missionary journey, knowing Apaches were still in the area and causing trouble. Fortunately, it was a short ride on in to Nogales and they got in before dark. They found a boarding house, got some food, and settled in for a well-deserved night's sleep. During the night, Pablo had a vision. There stood a man of Nogales, Mexico pleading with him and saying, "¡ven aquí y ayúdanos!" which means "come over and help us." This convinced Pablo that God had indeed called him to proclaim the good news to the people of Mexico.

The next morning, he shared his story with Kate and she agreed to follow his lead. Pablo and Kate obediently crossed the border into Mexico, and was amazed at the kindred spirit he felt with the people of Nogales. The town was newly founded and there was general excitement in the air. Pablo found it easy to talk with the people about the amazing story of Jim Caldwell's resurrection, and his own experience on the road to Tucson. He explained about his former name of Jose Maria Perez, and how his name change to Pablo was a testimony to the change in his heart, life, mind, body and soul.

The people were listening intently, so Kate shared her story of loose living and being the woman of a notorious criminal. They were fascinated with the stories, and the completely changed lives, but their culture made it difficult to be forgiving toward women. It must have been a God thing, because in spite of Kate's past, they soon they had a following of Caldwellians. Over the next few days, Pablo was careful to explain that they weren't to be following himself, nor Kate, nor Jim Caldwell, but a new movement of the Holy Spirit of God, which was the spirit of Jim.

Pablo and Kate spent several weeks with this new community, then returned to Tucson. There they spent time with Tommie, Junior, and Thad and shared stories of the ways God was moving in the lives of the new Caldwellians. Some wonderful and heartfelt stories were shared about changing lives toward serving and loving others, and other stories were offered about the troubles and insults they incurred. Pablo decided Tucson was a tougher place to spread the word, because he surprisingly had nothing but good things to report from Nogales. Plenty of challenging times were to come, but Pablo's short stay in Nogales with Kate was enjoyable and uplifting.

Pablo kept feeling the Holy Spirit nudging him to return to Mexico, so he told them that he needed to be moving on. Kate was glad he wasn't having to put up with any of the original twelve, and she decided she didn't want to either. Rather than staying with Tommie, Junior, and Thad, she decided to team up with Rose. She was back in Tucson and they all agreed she could probably use some company, considering the unwelcome advances she received from the unsavory magician Alexander Herrman.

The five of them gathered in a small circle, standing with arms around each other's shoulders, and heads bent toward the floor. They prayed for one another's safety and success and continued guidance from Jim's spirit. Pablo then packed up the bare minimum of supplies needed for a lengthy sojourn, and went on a yearlong missionary journey, establishing Caldwellian communities at each place he visited. He felt bad

# The Value of the Diamond

about abandoning the plan to do the work on horseback, but his calling to Mexico demanded the use of stagecoach and train, due to the excessive distances. Come to think of it, he felt pretty good about abandoning the plan because it was Pedro's.

He first rode horseback through Nogales, and warmly greeted his beloved community. After a short visit, he took a stagecoach to Chihuahua for a couple of months. His next stop by train was to Mexico City, where he enjoyed a lengthy stay, then a stagecoach to Guadalajara. Finally, he took a train to Monterrey, where he had considerable difficulties, which will be shared later in this story. Pablo became quite well known throughout Mexico, which proved useful in several ways.

Communities he founded started having questions, and the first telegram made it to him from Nogales, after he ultimately settled in Mexico City. Well, maybe not so much settled as jailed. He ran into the same problems with Catholic priests as he did in Phoenix, and he was sentenced to three years in jail for spreading fake news. Here are the questions Pablo received from those good people, translated into English.

PABLO (ALIAS JOSE MARIA PEREZ)

HELP!!!
HOW DO WE DEAL WITH PERSECUTION?
WILL JIM CALDWELL COME BACK TO EARTH?
WILL YOU BE COMING BACK TO NOGALES?

LOVINGLY,
THE CALDWELLIANS OF NOGALES

# The Value of the Diamond

Pablo was disappointed, but not surprised, that they were having troubles. He thought back to the three days that he was blind, when Jim's spirit taught him of the problems needing endurance, so he decided to write them a letter. His time in Mexico City was profitable for the kingdom, because he found Timoteo, a good man who could strengthen and encourage the Nogalesites in the challenges ahead. Timoteo was a vibrant young man who heard Pablo speak on one of his first days in Mexico City. When Timoteo heard the story about Pablo's road to Tucson experience, something came alive inside him. Pablo baptized him, and the very next day he was arrested. Timoteo visited him every day in jail to learn more about living the Caldwellian life. He pulled up a chair by Pablo's cell and they shared and learned and grew closer each day.

A rather divine thing happened next. The Mexican Central Railway linked Mexico City to Ciudad Juarez, and opened in March, 1884. As soon as Pablo finished his letter in jail, he waited for Timoteo's daily visit.

"Timoteo," announced Pablo upon his arrival, "the Lord has great need for you."

"It would be my honor to serve the Lord in any way he might need," responded a smiling Timoteo.

"Good," said Pablo, returning a smile. "I have received a telegram with questions from my friends in Nogales, and have finished my response. Now I need you to take it to them and stay as long as they need to help them figure out how to be faithful followers in the good times and the bad times."

Timoteo was hesitant at first. He was serious about helping in any way, but what would he do about money? Pablo talked a little bit about the idolatry of money, then a lot about faith, saying, "The Lord will provide, Timoteo. This is what the Lord wants you to do. The right people will come along at the right time to keep you sustained. Trust in the Lord."

"So why not," asked Timoteo, "send a telegram?"

Pablo explained, "This kind of thing needs a person there to answer their questions."

Feeling inspired, he took the envelope through the jail cell bars. As he pulled it toward himself, Pablo reached out his other hand with a closed fist. Timoteo was confused, but Pablo said, "Here, take this. It will get you on the train."

As Timoteo reached out his other hand, palm up, Pablo opened his fist. A surprising amount of pesos fell into Timoteo's hand, and with a shocked look on his face, he asked,"How?"

Pablo smiled and said, "The Lord works in mysterious ways. Just be thankful. I'll be praying for your journey."

Timoteo headed for the train depot with a buoyant feeling. He bought a ticket with some of the money Pablo gave him, boarded the train, and headed out for his important trip. Including stops, the train would take two days just to get to Ciudad Juarez, then another 346 miles to Nogales by way of stagecoach. Timoteo had plenty of time to read and think about Pablo's epistle to them, and he carried a handwritten copy of the telegram of questions they sent. Timoteo also felt the disappointment Pablo had for them, and was excited to get some answers to the good people of Nogales. Timoteo opened the letter so he could properly prepare himself for his visit. Here's how the letter began.

"To the community of believers in Nogales. Grace to you and peace." That felt good, because Timoteo knew Pablo truly wanted to impart peace to them, and further knew that the way to get there was through grace. The letter continued, "I give thanks to God for all of you, and mention you in my prayers.

# The Value of the Diamond

Your work of faith, labor of love, and steadfastness of hope is a testimony of the Holy Spirit working in your lives." Timoteo smiled this time, because he knew Pablo meant that, too. Even though Pablo had only spent a short amount of time with them, it was enough to know that they were genuine people and sincere Caldwellians.

Timoteo then continued reading. "It is with great sadness that I hear of your persecution. Know that your way of dealing with it is an example to all the believers in the state of Sonora. And your faith in God shines forth everywhere people talk about you. For it is already known how you welcomed me, turned to God, and wait for Jim, whom God raised from the dead."

Pablo then poured his heart out into the letter. "You yourselves know, 'mi familia,' that my coming to you was not in vain. And your speaking about the Holy Spirit and Jim Caldwell, is not to please mortals, but to please God. I deeply care for you, which is why I shared not only the good news, but also about myself. I thank God that you have received God's word, and the words of Jim Caldwell, who became God's son by resurrection from the dead."

Next, Pablo answered their question about persecution. "Your suffering for being Caldwellians is the same suffering you endured from your compatriots before I shared the good news with you. Your lovely, new town has attracted many bad hombres; they displease God, and have constantly been filling up the measure of their sins. Know that I have longed to see you again, but evil blocked my way. While I have been unable to return, my joy remains, and so must yours. Joy comes from the constant presence of the Spirit of Jim, because his peace and happiness are within, not dependent upon the things that happen around us."

# The Value of the Diamond

Timoteo paused from his reading, and found himself shedding tears about many things. Most importantly, it tore at his heart that the Nogalesites were being persecuted. He read over and over again from the telegram, the simple word "HELP!!!" He was glad that Pablo answered their question about dealing with persecution, and prayed for their understanding. He knew it would not be an easy response to be an example to others when treated poorly. Timoteo thought back to the time when he was mistreated in Mexico City. It was just after he met Pablo and became a Caldwellian. His own family disowned him for leaving the Catholic Church, so he well knew the challenge of dealing with feelings of loss and abandonment for your faith.

However, the letter brought tears of joy when he read how much Pablo loved them. He rejoiced that Pablo referred to the Nogalesites as 'mi familia,' and prayed their families would accept their decision to become Caldwellians. Timoteo remembered talking to Pablo about them, and was amazed that he used motherly language. Pablo said something about being gentle, as if he were caring for his own children, and that he cared for them deeply. It's the kind of language Pablo said he could never use when he was Jose Maria Perez, but Pablo was a totally different person. He said that he even urged the Nogalesites, in a fatherly way, to lead a Godly life.

After composing himself, Timoteo read on. "I have decided to remain in Mexico City, and I am sending Timoteo to you." Timoteo was curious about Pablo leaving out the fact that he was staying in Mexico City because he was in jail, but after a short pause, he continued reading, "His task is to strengthen and encourage you in your faith, so you won't be shaken by these persecutions. You know this is what you were destined

# The Value of the Diamond

for, as I told you when I was with you, and sadly it has become true. Continue to stand firm in the truth of resurrection, as Jim Caldwell has revealed, and as he spoke to me after his death. Therefore, build one another up in the boundless love it brings, and the eternal hope that it shares. You must not fight among yourselves, because there are plenty of enemies from outside the church." Timoteo put the letter down for a moment, as the enormity struck him about his task of strengthening and encouraging the Caldwellians.

After a while, he continued reading. "Finally, my children, I urge you in the name of Jim Caldwell, to live a life pleasing to God. Stay away from fornication, as is so prominent throughout North America. Control yourselves, so as not to give in to lustful passion like the bad hombres who do not know God. For God did not call us to impurity, but to holiness. Now concerning how to love one another. Let me make it even more difficult—love everyone, as Jim taught while he was here on earth. Meanwhile, live quietly, mind your own affairs, behave properly toward outsiders and be dependent on no one."

Timoteo paused again from his reading. He had to think about how he would answer the Nogalesites about loving outsiders while trying to stay away from them. He found himself wishing that he could have met Jim Caldwell, or even have a Pablo-type road to Tucson experience. But then again, he was happy to have been raised Catholic, and not need a dramatic change in his life. About then Timoteo felt his heart strangely warmed. A peace that passes all understanding filled his heart, mind, and soul, and all of a sudden he felt the answer was to be in the world but not of the world. His mind was spinning as he wondered where that came from, and just as quick, he knew it was an experience with the holy. Was it he spirit of Jim speaking to his heart or the Holy Spirit of God? He didn't know, and he didn't need to know, he just felt ready to share Good News with the struggling Nogalesites.

After a short rest to clear his mind, he read on. "So what about those who have died? Since we believe that Jim died and rose again, be filled with hope. For those who believe in eternal life, can never be beat. No matter what happens, we will enjoy a final victory. As for your question about Jim Caldwell coming back to earth, he will descend from heaven and we will be caught up in the clouds together with him to be taken to heaven forever. Therefore, encourage one another with these words." Timoteo smiled as he realized that his job of encouragement just go a little easier, thanks to Pablo.

"Now concerning the question of when? It will come like a thief in the night." Timoteo felt a twinge of concern at this comment, but luckily he read on. "That should not concern you, beloved, for you are not in darkness, you are children of light. So keep sober and aware of your actions by filling yourselves with faith, love, and hope. Therefore I encourage you to build one another up. So, mi familia, be at peace among yourselves. Admonish the idle, encourage the fainthearted, help the weak, and always be patient." All of a sudden the letter was speaking to Timoteo, as he had terrible troubles with patience. "Pray without ceasing, give thanks in all things but not for all things."

Timoteo loved that thought. What a great difference a simple idea makes. Timoteo knew he wasn't thankful for all things, because there are so many bad things happening all the time. But learning to be thankful in all things, to Timoteo, meant to look for good in spite of troubles. It was just such a delightful way to fix one's mind on positives. He smiled and read on. "Do not quench the Spirit. Hold fast to what is good and abstain from all evil. I solemnly command you to read this letter to our family. One final thought: your job is not to understand 'the meaning of life' but to live 'a life of meaning.' The grace of Jim and the power of God be with you."

Timoteo could hardly wait to get to his destination. It had already been a long train ride, and he still had a long stagecoach journey ahead. His mind was reeling with the thoughts at the end of Pablo's letter, but he was finally getting sleepy. As the train rattled down the track, the rhythmic sounds and feelings beckoned him to sleep. His mind was foggy now, but he still wondered about the last question in the telegram. Pablo shared no plans to return to Nogales, but Timoteo didn't want to leave them with any concerns, because he was going there to build them up. His inadequacy happily seemed to melt away as he drifted off to sleep.

The next day the train arrived in Ciudad Juarez. Timoteo felt a little lost because he had never been out of Mexico City. The city also seemed a little lost, having just changed its name from El Paso Del Norte, and was still having growing pains after the arrival of the Mexican Central Railway. The first person he asked for directions, helpfully guided him to the stagecoach stop. Once there, he bought a ticket for his lengthy trip on in to Nogales. Exhausted, he fell asleep for the rest of the journey.

The coach came to an abrupt stop, and Timoteo was amazed to find he had reached his destination. Nogales was a small town and he quickly found the Caldwellian congregation. Pablo thoughtfully arranged to have a telegraph message sent to the Nogalesites, so they were expecting him. Timoteo was overwhelmed with their hospitality and had a wonderful time in their midst. He was even surprised to be led by Jim's spirit many times during his lengthy visit. Pablo had taught him to keep his

# The Value of the Diamond

heart, mind, and soul open to the presence of Jim's spirit. For Timoteo, he sensed that presence by a chill going up his spine. For others, it was a matter of feeling the heart being strangely warmed. For all, it is about clearing the mind, to give room for God's presence.

————

A few months later, Timoteo was back in Mexico City. On his first visit to Pablo, who was still in jail, another telegram arrived. They gave it to Timoteo since he was heading back to see Pablo, who opened it immediately. It was from the churches Pablo founded on his missionary journey to Chihuahua. Pablo was visibly upset when he read the short question, and immediately commissioned Timoteo to transport a letter to them. "Oh, great! Another trip," Timoteo said with a laugh, but Pablo was in no mood for humor. Here's the telegram.

---

SEÑOR PABLO,

DO WE NEED TO FOLLOW HEBREW LAW
TO PROPERLY FOLLOW JIM?

WITH CONCERN,
THE CALDWELLIANS OF CHIHUAHUA

---

Pablo wrote so fast and furious that he had to rewrite his letter to the Chihuahuan Caldwellians, just to make it legible.

# The Value of the Diamond

He was hearing stories since his visit, that other Caldwellians arrived who were not about to ignore the laws in the Scriptures. Of all things, they were demanding that the Chihuahuan converts follow the laws of Abund. Pablo wondered if these poorly taught missionaries ever heard some of Jim's responses about the law. One story Pablo heard was when Jim was asked about the law of an eye for an eye, and he responded "Do you always do exactly what the law says?" Pablo's mouth slowly turned into a wry smile as he realized the importance of his letter to the Chihuahan Caldwellians, and he wasn't happy until his third attempt.

Once the letter was done, he gave it to Timoteo with a bit more money. It seems the local Caldwellians were helping to support Pablo during his time in jail. Timoteo then boarded the train for another two-day journey. Even though Chihuahua was closer than Nogales, it was still about 900 miles away. The great thing was that Chihuahua was an actual stop on the way to Ciudad Juarez, so he didn't need a stagecoach trip at the end of these travels. As he sat back for another important journey, he began to read what Pablo had to say this time. His curiosity had certainly been piqued from Pablo's furious writing.

"I, Pablo, was sent neither by human commission nor from human authorities, but through Jim Caldwell and God the Father, who raised him from the dead." Timoteo paused and wished he, too, had a divine commission, but settling for a commission from Pablo wasn't too bad either.

"To the Churches of Chihuahua: Grace to you and peace. Always remember Jim Caldwell, who gave himself to set us free from the present evil age." Timoteo could relate to the present evil age, and even more so to the freedom he found in becoming a Caldwellian. "I am angry." All of a sudden Timoteo wasn't too sure this would be an easy letter to deliver. "Why would you even consider turning to a different gospel? There is no other gospel. You are being confused by people who want to pervert the good news of the resurrection of Jim Caldwell." Wow. Timoteo had heard of these problems, but he had hoped it wasn't true. "Listen. If anyone proclaims a different gospel, let them be accursed! The gospel I proclaim is not of human origin, I received it through a direct revelation of Jim. When God was pleased to reveal his Son in me, so that I might proclaim him among the Mexicans, I did not confer with any human being. In what I am writing to you, before God, I do not lie!"

Timoteo's eyes were wide open as he read on. "To bring clarification, I went to Phoenix and laid before the leaders the gospel that I proclaim among the Mexicans. When they saw that I had been entrusted with the gospel for this purpose, they acknowledged that I was Pedro's counterpart, who then took the gospel to the United States of America. When the recognized pillars, Jimbo and Pedro and Johnny, saw the good work I was doing, they extended the right hand of fellowship. We had already agreed to this distribution of work, but missionary trouble-makers were planting seeds of doubt. Then they asked that I remember the poor, which was what I was eager to do."

Timoteo was impressed with the letter so far. Pablo had offered a direct answer to their question about following law first, before becoming a Caldwellian. It was a clear and resounding "no." Timoteo recalled how hot under the collar Pablo was when the telegram arrived in Mexico City, and expected it to be a difficult response. Actually, it was challenging, because Pablo went on to attack Pedro, one who followed Jim during his time on earth. It seems the two of them

# The Value of the Diamond

met one time after their ministries began, and Pablo opposed Pedro to his face. Pablo was incensed that Pedro properly ate with people who had not become people of the faith in their ways, then stopped for fear of a growing faction who demanded following the laws. But Pablo said that Pedro was not acting consistently with the truth of the gospel. He then succinctly summarized the problem, and said to Pedro, "If you don't live like a like a person of faith, how can you compel anyone to live the life of faith?" Then Timoteo continued reading with satisfaction.

"A person is justified not by the works of the law but through faith in Jim Caldwell. I died to the law, so that I might live to God. It is no longer I who live, but it is Jim who lives in me." Timoteo really liked that, because he could feel the spirit of Jim in his heart, mind, and soul, then continued reading. "I do not nullify the grace of God; for if righteousness comes through the law, then Jim died for nothing. You foolish Chihuahans, quit acting like a small, whiny dog! The only thing I want to learn from you is this: Did you receive the Spirit by doing the works of the law or by believing what you heard? Just as Aapo 'believed God, it was counted as righteousness,' then those who believe are also counted as righteous. That's you, without following the laws of the Scriptures!" Timoteo felt ready, right then and there, to be talking to the Caldwellians. Then he frowned, because he knew he had a long trip ahead of him, so he returned to the letter.

"Mis hermanitos y hermanitas of faith, my point is that the law, which came 430 years after Aapo, was not needed for him to be justified. It was faith. Is the law then opposed to the promises of God? Certainly not! The law was simply our disciplinarian until Jim came, so that we might be justified by faith. But now that faith has come, we no longer need a disciplinarian. In the name of Jim Caldwell, we are all children of God through faith." Timoteo nearly jumped out of his seat with agreement and yelled "hallelujah!" then looked around with embarrassment before reading on. "There is no longer Mexican or American, there is no longer slave or free, there is no longer male and female; for we are all one in Jim. And if you belong to Jim, then you are Aapo's offspring, heirs according to promise."

Timoteo's head was spinning. This letter was so much heavier than the first one he carried to the Nogalesites. Being raised Catholic, Timoteo had an appreciation for the Scriptures, but knew little about them. And here was Pablo arguing against the laws of God. Timoteo had heard that Jim preached support of the law, other than it needed expanded. Timoteo was mentally exhausted. He didn't quite get all this talk about Aapo, so he closed his eyes and rested for a while. He eventually drifted off to sleep wondering how he could respond to the Chihuahuan's questions. He soon woke back up, realized he had no answers, and decided to continue reading.

"Answer me this, you who desire to be subject to the law. Aapo had two sons, one by Beatrice and one by her maid. The maid's child was born according to the ways of the world, while Beatrice's child was born through the promise. So, would you rather be a part of promise or a part of the world? The only thing that counts is faith working through love. Who prevented you from obeying the truth? But whoever it is that is confusing you will pay the penalty. I wish they would castrate themselves!" Oh, my! Timoteo was surprised with Pablo. Was he being too honest? With that thought, he read on. "For you were called to freedom, which can be summed up in a single commandment, 'You shall love your neighbor as yourself.'"

# The Value of the Diamond

Timoteo liked having a summary statement. The problem was that he felt free to not love his neighbor. For that matter, he certainly struggled with loving himself. He then hoped Pablo had something useful coming up. Looking back down at the letter, he saw, "Live by the Spirit so you are not subject to the law. Now the works of the world are obvious: fornication, impurity, recklessness, idolatry, sorcery, enmities, strife, jealousy, anger, quarrels, dissensions, factions, envy, drunkenness, carousing, and things like these. They do not lead to the kingdom of God. Here's what does: love, joy, peace, patience, kindness, generosity, faithfulness, gentleness, and self-control. So if you choose to live by the Spirit, you must also be guided by the Spirit."

Timoteo really liked this. He was glad Pablo didn't just list the works of the world, he followed it with the works of the kingdom. He was finally getting some ideas how he could talk with the Chihuahuans. If they brought up troubles, he could discuss their worldly ways. If they asked about spiritual things, he could chat about Pablo's list of the things that lead one to the kingdom of God. He was starting to get excited now, because his stop was only a few hours away. It was also great that he would be able to get off the train and be at his destination without need of any stagecoach travel, so he continued to read.

"When fellow Caldwellians sin, be forgiving in a spirit of gentleness. Bear one another's burdens, because Caldwellianism is not an isolated way to practice faith. Do not be deceived, for what you reap is what you sow. Do not grow weary in doing what is right. Whenever you have an opportunity, work for the good of all. Never boast about anything except Jim and his resurrection. Always remember that being a new creation is everything! As for those who follow this rule—peace be upon them. I have one last thought as I prepare to send you this letter with Timoteo. Faith isn't perfect, we all make mistakes, but grace is perfect because it comes from God."

Timoteo wished he could pull out a pen and add one more thought to the end of the letter, but he knew he couldn't. He felt somehow that this letter was going to be remembered. Anyway, what he wanted to add was that anyone who truly seeks perfection, has to add imperfection. Perfection is about completeness, which means that perfection is not complete without imperfection. It was a great lesson he heard one time from a Chinese friend. It helped him to solve the perfectionism problem he was raised with. His friend had said that you will always fail to be perfect, so embrace imperfection and feel complete.

Timoteo had a satisfying sigh as he closed the letter. He knew it would be difficult, but he was overjoyed how well Pablo dealt with everything. Well, not everything. He didn't have Timoteo's piece about perfectionism, but so be it. At least it was a part of his own spiritual life. As the train clanged to a halt, the conductor called out, "All off, heading for Chihuahua." Timoteo gathered up his meager supplies, offered a quick word of thanks, and began asking those at the stop where he could find a Caldwellian Church.

# ACT II
## NO DIVIDING WALL

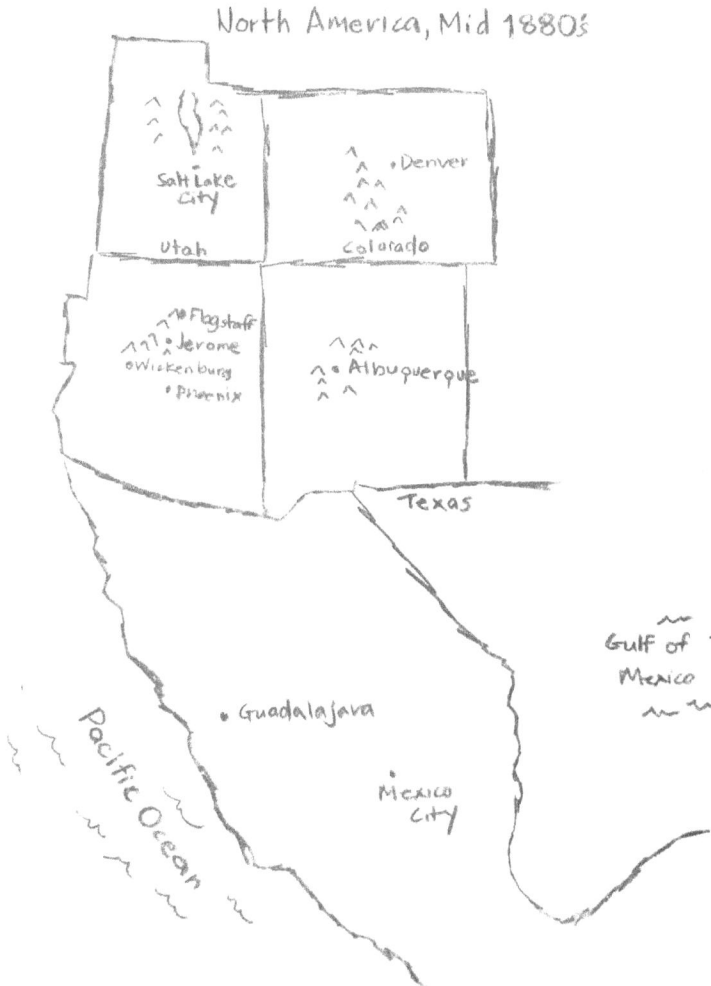

North America, Mid 1880's

# The Value of the Diamond

## SCENE ONE
### Planting Seeds

Back in the American Southwest, there was a Russian man who practiced the Orthodox faith, who married a woman who wasn't religious. He had fallen deeply in love with her, which helped to overcome their differing world views. After the Russian Invasion was over, they settled in Wickenburg. He was well liked, and went by the name of Hank. The town certainly had its share of problems: the Apache Wars didn't end until 1886, there were mine closures, desperados, drought, and a disastrous flood in 1890 when the Walnut Creek Dam burst. In spite of all these troubles, Wickenburg continued to grow, and in 1895 the railroad arrived.

Hank was a devout man who gave generously to those in need, and prayed constantly to God. One afternoon he had a vision of an angel calling his name. He was nearly paralyzed in terror, but managed to eke out the words "What is it, Lord?" The angel responded with "Take the 3:10 to Yuma, and find a man named Pedro," so Hank immediately obeyed. About noon the next day, as Hank was looking around Yuma, Pedro began to pray. He fell into a trance, and saw the heavens open up and a large sheet came down. Inside it were rattlesnakes and gila monsters, and roadrunners and quail, then a voice said, "Get up, Pedro; kill and eat." But Pedro said, "I prefer tortillas and frijoles. I quit killing after I became a follower of Jim." The voice then said, "Not my point," then the sheet rose back to heaven.

To say the least, Pedro was puzzled, then he heard Hank outside calling for him. While Pedro was still thinking about the vision, the voice said, "A man named Hank is outside. Go say,

# The Value of the Diamond

'I am the one you are looking for. Why are you here?'" After Pedro did as instructed, Hank said "I was directed by an angel to come for you." Pedro was taken aback, but seeing that Hank wasn't carrying a gun, he continued to listen. "The angel said I am supposed to bring you to my house and to hear what you have to say." So the first thing Pedro did was invite him in, and give him dinner and lodging for the night.

The following day Pedro and Hank traveled back to Wickenburg. They took the train, and ended up having a useful chat. Hank couldn't get over the fact that the angel called him to hear what Pedro had to say, thinking that Pedro might be an angel himself. Pedro laughed more than he had in a while, and said "Maybe you're the angel! You did what the angel told you to do." Hank was quick to reply, "So did you." After that they agreed that they were both men of God, then shared their stories. Hank loved how Pedro became a new man from following Jim, and Pedro had no idea Russia had an Orthodox Church.

When they arrived at Hank's home in Wickenburg, they found that many had assembled. Pedro looked around and saw a lot of Russian mementos, then he spoke. "You know that Americans are not fond of Russians, and Hank tells me his wife is not religious." The crowd shifted uneasily, until Pedro gave a friendly smile. "But God showed me a vision that took me until now to get its point. I am most pleased to let you know that God was telling me, it's okay to be in fellowship with Russians and nonbelievers." Clapping rang out for a long time, then he continued. "So when Hank came for me, even though I didn't understand then, I came without objection. Hank said that I am supposed to have something to say to you, so believe me, I've thought and prayed about this for a long time. I didn't get much inspiration, so I guess I'll just speak from the heart."

Then Pedro began. "I think the vision has taught me the great lesson that it doesn't matter to God where we came from or what we have done." Again the house rang out with applause and appreciative smiles. "In every nation, including Russia, anyone who loves God and does what is right is acceptable to him."

Hank then asked, "How about my wife?"

Pedro thought for a moment and said, "She just doesn't know the unconditional love of God, but God knows her and loves her. In fact, Jim Caldwell came to preach peace and wholeness to all. That message has spread throughout the Arizona Territory, beginning in Phoenix where Jim was baptized. Then God anointed Jim with the Holy Spirit and with power. The difference is that people have been baptized by nearly every religion in the world, but our joy comes in receiving the Holy Spirit."

Everyone's eyes and ears were transfixed on Pedro as he continued. "Jim went about doing good things and making people's lives better, and I witnessed all that he did. My brother and I were the first people he called to follow him, and believe me, I didn't know that unconditional love of God when I was called. But there was something amazing about his eyes, because they were so full of peace. As he attracted crowds, he began to teach about a new way of life. Then he got a visit from some heavenly beings who told him the Russians were going to hang him."

Everyone's eyes were wide open, but Pedro assured them that it was all a part of God's plan. "They put him to death by hanging him from a noose, but God raised him on the third day. He appeared to us and commanded us to preach that he was ordained by God." While Pedro was still speaking, the Holy Spirit fell on all who heard the word. Some fell on their knees and began praying, while others raised their hands and shouted words of joy and celebration. Pedro was astonished that the gift of the Holy Spirit had been poured out on Russians and nonbelievers alike. Then he thought, "Do I have any right to withhold the water for baptizing these people who have already received the Holy Spirit?" So he baptized them in the name of Jim Caldwell.

Now the rest of the disciples who were in Arizona heard that Russians and nonbelievers had accepted the word of God, so when Pedro went back to Phoenix, he was criticized. They angrily asked, "Why did you even go into the house of a Russian and his nonbelieving wife?" Pedro began to explain, step by step, all that had happened. He even mentioned that the Spirit told him to make no distinction, and that the Spirit told Hank his entire household would be saved. Then Pedro said, "As I began to speak, the Holy Spirit fell on them, just as it had upon us at the beginning. And I remembered Jim saying, 'The Dipper baptized with water, but you will be baptized with the Holy Spirit.' If then God gave them the gift he gave us, how could I hinder God?" And they praised God, saying, "Then God has given even to the Russians and nonbelievers, the repentance that leads to life."

Now those who were scattered, because of the persecution that took place when Jack became the first martyr, traveled as far away as the New Mexico Territory, Colorado, the Utah Territory, Nevada, and California. They worked at evangelizing nonbelievers, and the hand of the Lord was with them. A great number became believers and turned to God concerning his risen son Jim Caldwell. News of this came to the church in Phoenix, and when they heard about the grace of God spreading throughout America, they prayed that the new believers would remain faithful to the Lord with steadfast devotion.

---

When Pablo was finally released from jail in Mexico City, he sensed God calling him back to Jerome, up in the Arizona Territory. He certainly had his ups and downs in Mexico, so maybe a break from that mission was just what he needed. He booked a train trip to Nogales, visited his friends there, and then headed straight past Phoenix. He heard the church in Phoenix was getting more and more organized by some of the original Twelve, and wasn't excited about their administration. Pablo knew his divine calling to mission work, and didn't want to get slowed down by their tiresome ways. Especially if Pedro had anything to do with it.

The Caldwellian Church of Phoenix had moved out of the Catholic Church, and was getting to be known far and wide. When they heard that Pablo was in Jerome, they decided to have him go do some mission work at the new church start in Flagstaff. They chose Colton, a new believer with great enthusiasm for the faith, to go to Jerome to look for Pablo. When he found him, he announced, "Pedro says you have to go with me to help the new church start in Flagstaff." This met Pablo's ears like chalk scratching on blackboard, but he also was trying to be open to God.

After a bit of discussion, Pablo and Colton mounted their horses and were on their way to Flagstaff. It was for an entire

# The Value of the Diamond

year that they stayed with the church and taught them what Pablo knew about the risen Lord. One day, a traveler came to Flagstaff from Wickenburg, and told them of the terrible flood of 1890 and the ensuing drought and famine. The disciples determined that according to their ability, each would send relief to the believers throughout the Arizona Territory. This they did by sending it to the church leaders by Colton and Pablo, who traveled several times in the next year.

---

About that time, Marshal Garfias turned his anger toward the Caldwellians in Phoenix, and became increasingly violent. He wanted to come across as tougher than the Russian General Dmitri Ivanov had been, so he had Jimbo, the brother of Johnny, dragged to his office. After all, that's how Pablo, formerly known as Jose Maria Perez, had treated the believers at first, until his road to Tucson experience. When Jimbo arrived, the marshal was obviously not in a good mood. He demanded to know if Jimbo was trying to take away his power, but Jimbo didn't answer. "You causing trouble like Jim Caldwell did?" Again, no answer. Now the marshal was furious and said, "I ain't gonna hang ya like Dmitri did to Jim, so here's this." He then pulled his gun out of its holster and shot and killed Jimbo. As Jimbo's body hit the office floor, dust scattered, along with the deputies who brought him in.

Word got around about that terrible event, and the marshal was surprised to find that people were pleased. It was almost as if, the meaner he got the more popular he became. He decided to go after Pedro next, the ring leader, but only had him arrested, because he knew that Pedro had a large following. The main Caldwellian home church in Phoenix prayed fervently to God for his safety, not knowing anything else they could do. Pedro was bound with two chains, guards on either side of him, and guards at the front of the door to his cell. The jail floor was nothing but dirt and desert sand, and the room was dark, having no windows. Suddenly an angel of the Lord appeared and a light shone in the cell. The angel woke Pedro and told him to get up quickly. Pedro stood up and the chains fell off his wrists, then the angel told him to put on his sandals. As he was doing that, the angel told him to wrap his cloak around himself and said, "Follow me."

Pedro remembered when Jim said the same thing to him, so he complied. It's somehow those kinds of moments when you just know that following means never turning back. After they passed the sleeping guards, they came to an iron gate. It opened for them of its own accord, and they went outside, when suddenly the angel left. Pedro thought, "Now I am sure that the Lord has sent his angel and rescued me from the hands of the marshal." He then went to a house church where people had been praying for him, and knocked on the door.

It was the middle of the night, so there was no motion inside. He knocked again and finally heard some stirring. It was the maid, who cautiously went to the door and asked, "Who's there?" When he responded, she recognizing Pedro's voice, and was so overjoyed that instead of opening the door, she ran in and announced that Pedro was standing outside. He thought, "that sure reminds me of one of the teachings on the hillside Jim shared about 'knock and the door will be opened for you,'" yet nobody was opening the door! He continued to wait as people were obviously getting up.

# The Value of the Diamond

Inside the house, the people were saying to the maid, "You are out of your mind!" but she insisted it was true. Meanwhile, Pedro started knocking at the door again, and when they finally came to see what was going on, they all recognized his voice. Being greatly amazed when they let him in, he motioned with his hand to be quiet. After all he had just escaped jail, so they quietly brought him in. Pedro then told them how the Lord brought him out of the jail, and they were deeply encouraged that God was still doing great things. Pedro then encouraged them to fully share his story with all the believers, saying "my story of faith in the face of obstacles is your story, too. Just not with the same people. There are those who will hate you because of your faith, but the outcome is still the same." After a quick nap, he left before daybreak.

Now when Marshal Garfias got up that morning, he was sipping his coffee and feeling great that Pedro was successfully behind bars. He was sitting back in his favorite chair with his feet comfortably resting on the edge of the desk. The serenity of that moment was soon interrupted when a jailer frantically knocked at his door, and gave him the bad news that Pedro had escaped. The marshal nearly fell out of his chair, spilled his coffee all over himself, and was beyond furious.

He jumped up and ran to the jail, and to his disbelieving eyes he found the gate open. When he looked in, he saw the two chains laying on the floor, and he felt sick to his stomach. He angrily asked the guards, "Who let Pedro out?" The guards claimed innocence, but it was obvious that Pedro couldn't have gotten out on his own. The marshal asked "Who has the key for the chains?" and again the guards said they didn't have it, and they didn't know where it was. He quickly touched his pocket to make sure he didn't have it either, and to his shock and

# The Value of the Diamond

embarrassment, there they were. Now the marshall was far too proud to admit it, so he stared at them in the kind of way no one wants to get stared at. The two guards who were supposed to be on either side of Pedro, and the guards who were at the front door, knew they were in trouble. One guard suggested it was an act of God, so the marshal said "Maybe this is, too!" Garfias then drew his gun and shot and killed all four guards, right then and there. He didn't need any witnesses, in caseone of them noticed the key in his pocket. When Pedro got word of this, he made his way to Wickenburg and stayed there.

This story surprisingly made the marshal even more famous than he had been before. He thought the town's people would be angry, but they heard stories about how Pedro escaped with divine help. It turned out that they were impressed that he dared to arrest Pedro in the first place. Being of Mexican descent, he never expected acceptance in Phoenix in the first place, but his fame just kept growing. Tales of his heroics as a gunfighter when he first arrived were not only remembered but embellished. The marshal was so enamored with his growing fame, that he announced he would give a speech. When that day came, he was overjoyed to see a great crowd, probably the biggest gathering of people anyone had ever seen. To help with his short stature, and growing ego, he stood on a crate draped with a blanket to hide it.

As he was talking, the people were chanting, "The voice of a god! The voice of a god! The voice of a god!" This inflated Enrique's ego to biblical proportions, and he lapped up the praise as if it were earned. It was almost like Enrique tasted the forbidden fruit as Adam did, which says "of the tree of the knowledge of good and evil you shall not eat, for in the day that you eat of it you shall die" (Genesis 2:17). Well, Enrique was

# The Value of the Diamond

certainly chewing a nice juicy piece of ego fruit, when right in the middle of his speech, an angel of the Lord struck him down. Marshal Enrique Garfias clutched his chest, started choking, then fell off the crate and died. Meanwhile, the word of God continued to advance and gain believers.

———————

Now in the church in Flagstaff, there were many prophets and teachers. While they were worshiping the Lord and fasting, the Holy Spirit said, "Set apart for me Colton and Pablo for the work to which I have called them. To witness equality, have Kate and Rose come up from Tucson and join them." As soon as they arrived, the Caldwellian congregation laid their hands on the four of them and sent them off. The adventure became Pablo's missionary journey to North America. So, being sent out by the Holy Spirit, they first went to proclaim the word of God among the Havasupai Tribe of the Grand Canyon. Colton was a bit surprised at this choice, so Pablo admitted that he always wanted to see the Grand Canyon. The fact that the Havasupai Reservation had just been founded in 1880, made it even more intriguing, so the four of them headed northwest around the San Francisco Peaks and across the Coconino Plateau.

As they got closer, they took the short expedition north to see the Grand Canyon, and camped that night near the rim. Pablo was so excited that he barely got any sleep, was up well before dawn, walked carefully toward the edge, and sat down to await the view. It turned out to be better than anything he could have ever expected. As the sun slowly rose, his jaw gradually dropped. The mist dispersed with elegance, and the

# The Value of the Diamond

darkness was displaced with an almost eerie light. Pablo rose to his feet in awe, as the canyon walls first appeared, with their varying colors of orange and brown and green and yellow. Then the endless depths and distances of the valleys and peaks revealed their sublime majesty. The other three joined him, and Colton noticed tears in Pablo's eyes. He patted him on the shoulder and said, "Sure glad ya chose this place to visit."

After Rose and Kate agreed, Pablo composed himself and said "I heard about John Wesley Powell's Colorado River expedition here in 1869, and have wanted to see this place ever since. My joy is complete, because that incredible story is now a part of my memory." Colton smiled, and they all agreed that they gained a whole new appreciation of why the Indians of the area, who had been there for over 1,000 years, called it sacred ground.

Packing up their meager supplies, they headed west in search of the most remote community in the U.S. They had to leave their horses at the top of the Havasu Canyon, to take the long, and steep path eight miles below the rim of the Grand Canyon. Finally, they arrived at Supai Village. It was not common to have outsiders, so Pablo asked to see the Shaman. The Shaman expressed interest in hearing what Pablo had to say, but the chief got word of this and opposed the meeting.

Suddenly, Pablo was filled with the Holy Spirit, looked intently at the chief and said, "You son of the devil, you enemy of all righteousness, full of all deceit and villainy, will you not stop making crooked the straight paths of the Lord?" The chief was more surprised than anything, because Pablo was on the chief's territory. Then Pablo continued, "And now listen—the hand of the Lord is against you, and you will be blind for a while, unable to see the sun." Immediately mist and darkness came over him and he went about groping for someone to lead him by the hand.

The Shaman arrived just in time to see and hear all of this, and he was astonished, so he motioned for Pablo and Colton to come with him. The women wanted to go, but the Shaman said no. The three of them walked to the famous Havasu Falls, and the Shaman had a big smile of joy on his face as they arrived. He said to Pablo, "This is our paradise. The beautiful blue-green waters even gave us our name. We proudly call ourselves the Havasupai Tribe, which means 'People of the Blue-Green Water.' You two are very fortunate to be allowed to come here. It is sacred to us."

"Is that why you wouldn't let the women folk come?" asked Pablo. The Shaman did not answer, but soon enough they sat down in their idyllic setting. First they smoked a peace pipe, then the Shaman talked extensively about the ancient spirituality of the indigenous peoples. He shared about the soul and afterlife, the spirits and gods, and the sacred hoop of life. He explained that their ways were about honoring the connections of life, to the point of asking a twig for forgiveness when they needed to break it off to build a fire.

Pablo felt properly honored to be hearing these stories. He then followed by sharing the good news of Jim Caldwell and his resurrection, and how he himself was blind for three days while the risen Lord taught him. At that moment, Pablo was filled with the Holy Spirit, and asked the Shaman if he wanted to be baptized. They agreed that their spirituality seemed to fit together, so the Shaman agreed to baptized. The three of them waded out into the warm, soothing water and Pablo baptized him in the name of Jim Caldwell. As the Shaman rose from the water, he said he felt like he died and was reborn, much like the

# The Value of the Diamond

Shamanism that has been practiced for over 100,000 years.

They spent several days at this wonderful site, talking at length about their experiences. Finally, they shared prayers in celebration of this wondrous place, and mutual learnings, then returned to the village. The chief had has sight back and wasn't too happy to see Pablo and Colton. The Shaman calmed him down and told him about their experience by the Falls. Pablo and Colton then gathered Rose and Kate and bid their farewell. Once they got back to their horses at the top of the canyon, Colton asked, "Where now?" Pablo responded, "I hear interesting things about Salt Lake City" so they headed off for a lengthy journey north.

It proved to be a difficult and frustrating trip, trying to get around the Grand Canyon. Pablo knew the only way over the Colorado River was after they would be close to Nevada. He expected plenty of improvements, since Nevada became the 36th state in 1864, and they were more than delighted to find a bridge across the Black Canyon. After a while they rode into a small settlement with a structure that was built in 1855 by Mormon missionaries. Pablo wanted to stop and chat with the Mormons, but he felt the Holy Spirit calling him to go on up to Salt Lake City and see it for himself.

As the four pressed forward, they shared stories they heard about the City. They agreed that it was settled by the Latter-day Saints, and knew that Brigham Young was their leader. They further agreed that those pioneers were seeking religious freedom, but beyond that they knew nothing. That's when they decided to not talk further about things they didn't know. The time proved fruitful, as they got to know each other much better during their 400-mile journey to Salt Lake City.

Pablo said he would never forget the site when they first

# The Value of the Diamond

saw the City. He was beyond surprised to find out it had grown to a population of over 200,000, but that view of the City sitting against the majestic backdrop of the Wasatch Mountains was already worth the trip. They entered the city, and asked around for a guide of sorts to tell them about the metropolis. A nicely dressed young man shared six things he saw as important:

1. In 1846, the ill-fated Donner Party trekked across the valley through Emigration Canyon.
2. By 1857, there was a public outcry against the Church practice of polygamy.
3. Gold and silver was discovered in the Wasatch Mountains.
4. In 1869, the first transcontinental railroad was completed at Promontory Summit.
5. Bitter conflicts broke out between the LDS-controlled local government and Federal authorities.
6. To achieve statehood, the LDS Church agreed to ban polygamy.

Pablo said to him, "We would like to worship with an LDS church," so the young man directed them to a local chapel for a service. On the Sabbath day they went into the chapel and sat down. They were pleased to find a pleasant welcome and friendly worshipers. The service began with hymns and prayers, then the bishop looked at Pablo and Colton and said, "Brothers, if you have any word of exhortation, you are most welcome to give it now." So Pablo stood up and with a gesture began to speak.

"The God of our ancestors made the Mayans great during

their stay in the land of the Hondurans, then led them out. For forty years he put up with them in the wilderness." Most of the congregants laughed because they knew a patient God. "He then gave them their land as an inheritance, and later gave them judges until the time of the prophet Samuel. Then they asked for a king, and God gave them Saul, who reigned for forty years. Then he made Montezuma their king, and at long last God gave us Jim Caldwell. Before his coming, Jim's cousin was offering a baptism of repentance, asking, 'Who do you suppose that I am? I am not the savior, like the one who is coming after me.'

"You descendants of Aapo's family, and others who fear God, to us the message of this salvation has been sent. Because the residents of Phoenix and their leaders did not recognize him, they condemned him. Even though they found no cause for a sentence of death, they killed him. They took him down from the noose, and laid him in a former diamond mine for a tomb. But God raised him from the dead, and for many days he appeared to his followers, and they are now his witnesses. And we bring you now that good news. Let it be known to you, my brothers and sisters that through this man forgiveness of sins is proclaimed to you. In the name of Jim Caldwell, everyone who believes is set free from all those sins."

As Pablo and Colton were going out, the people urged them to speak about these things again the next Sabbath. When that day came around, thousands gathered to hear the word of the Lord. But when the bishop saw the crowds, he was filled with jealousy and contradicted what was spoken by Pablo. He began to talk of John Smith and the Book of Mormon, but Pablo tried to speak over him, saying, "It was necessary that the word of God should be spoken first to you. Since you reject it and judge yourself to be unworthy of eternal life, we are now turning to the nonbelievers."

When the unbelievers from the city heard this, they were glad and praised the word of the Lord, putting them on the road to eternal life. Thus the word of the Lord spread throughout the region. But the LDS members incited the devout women of high standing and the leading men of the city, and stirred up persecution against Pablo, Colton, Rose, and Kate, and drove them out of their region. So they shook the dust off their feet in protest against them, and departed. Kate was quite incensed, but Rose managed to calm her down. Soon Colton asked Pablo the now common question, "Where to now?" He responded, "I believe we are being called to go to Denver."

---

As they headed out for a grueling trip, Colton asked if there was any chance they could sell their horses and take the Transcontinental Railroad. Right then they found themselves within eyesight of the train depot. Colton declared it a sign, and Pablo agreed that it would be okay, because they all were developing back and shoulder troubles. It was easy selling their horses, and then they had plenty of money to take the train and buy horses again later, so they did it.

Getting on the train was a useful experience. It truly gained them insight into spreading God's word to a wider audience. Colton struck up a conversation with another traveler, who explained that "the railroad was originally a goal of President Abraham Lincoln. The route began in Omaha, Nebraska where the Union Pacific Railroad built westward, while the Central

# The Value of the Diamond

Pacific Railroad Company would start in Sacramento and build eastward. Each company received $48,000 in government bonds for every mile of track built. The Native Americans often attacked the workers, as they felt threatened by the progress of the white man and his 'iron horse' across their native lands." Colton was mesmerized by the story, so the man continued.

"Chinese laborers were hired and were toiling under brutal conditions to bring the line east. Irish immigrants and Civil War veterans were hired and started bringing the line west. The Central Pacific workers built huge wooden trestles to traverse canyons and they blasted tunnels through granite mountains. By1869, the two companies were working only miles from each other. They agreed to meet on Promontory Summit, just north of the Great Salt Lake, and on May 10 a Golden Spike was driven.

"I was there for the ceremony, and it was a great celebration for linking the Central Pacific and Union Pacific. A telegraph cable immediately went out to President Grant with the news that the transcontinental railroad had been completed." Colton asked how he knew so much, and he replied that he was the one who carried the message for the telegraph. After hearing a good story, Colton drifted off to sleep, happy that they weren't doing this part of the missionary journey on horseback. Pablo had also been listening, but he kept nodding off, while Kate and Rose were fast asleep.

As Denver slowly came into view, Colton got a bit homesick. It was one thing to be all the way up in Salt Lake City, but Denver was another 500 miles from his home. About that time the train whistle blew, and Colton felt lonely and tired and sorry for himself. As he shook off the sadness, the train came rolling to a stop and the four of them got off. It was a chilly day in the mile-high city, so they first looked for a boarding house to put them up for a while. They easily found a place and settled in with their few belongings, then headed out for a short stroll of the city. Soon Kate announced that her brother lived in nearby Redstone, Colorado and she wanted to go visit him.

"We're not going," Pablo flatly announced.

"Well, I think I am," countered Kate.

Colton was confused and asked, "Aren't we following the lead of the Spirit?"

"Yes," offered Kate,"and the Spirit is leading me to see my kin. What you don't know about me is that I was born in the Kingdom of Hungary as Maria Katalin Magdolna Horony. I miss my family, and I sense my destiny in that direction."

Rose had tears in her eyes and said, "We need to let her go," and at that, Big Nose Kate departed. She immensely enjoyed the visit with her brother, then started dating an Irish blacksmith from Aspen, Colorado. They got married on March 2, 1890, and after working mining camps in the area, they moved to Bisbee, Arizona where she ran a bakery. She left her life of missionary work, but continued to live the Caldwellian lifestyle. Her experiences with Jim Caldwell changed her, like coal into a diamond.

As the remaining three continued their walk, they were amazed at how fast America was growing. They realized that their isolated experiences in the Arizona Territory weren't a good barometer of life outside the desert. Denver had only been founded since 1858, but by 1890, it had grown to be the 26th largest city in America, and the fifth-largest city west of the Mississippi River. Manufacturing soared over this same period of time to $40 million, however this attracted other problems like crime and poverty. What was familiar was the rampant gambling, prostitution, and alcohol, which was in its early stages of fighting for prohibition.

This is what gave Pablo his initial inspiration. He heard people on the streets talking about the new Charity Organization Society, which coordinated services and fund raising for many agencies. He also found out that Myron Reed, pastor of the First Congregational Church, was questioning the Society's efforts to distinguish the "worthy" from the "unworthy" poor. Pablo returned that night with the decision to share the good news about Jim Caldwell to the people of Myron Reed's congregation.

The next morning Pablo, Colton, and Rose were filled with the Holy Spirit as they found the church, and the pastor was in. They sat in his office, and their zeal was so contagious, Pastor Reed invited Pablo to speak at his church on Sunday. Rose was also a great speaker, but the church wasn't open to women preaching. The pastor explained that they were interested in fighting injustice, but it became obvious he couldn't see it right under his nose. As they left the church, Rose asked, "Do you know what yer gonna say?" Pablo replied, "Of course not but I'm sure the spirit of Jim will guide me." Rose smiled at that thought as they returned to their boarding house.

Sunday morning couldn't come quick enough, because their missionary journey so far wasn't all smooth sailing. The Havasupai chief seemed to be a deterrent, but Pablo and Colton ended up having a great experience with the Shaman. The Mormon people were very open to Pablo's message, until the bishop opposed him. They wondered what the Congregational Church would have in store for them, so they spent the next few days in prayer and fasting. This renewed their energy, so they could fulfil God's purpose in their lives.

# The Value of the Diamond

At long last, they were making their way back to the church. It was a pleasant building, dominated by the charisma of the pastor. As they walked in, members proudly told them that Pastor Reed was not just their minister, he was also a lawyer and a political activist. Making their way toward the front, Pastor Reed hobbled toward them, so some parishioners explained that he was shot in the leg while serving in the Union Army. Colton looked at Pablo in a way that seemed to show deference, so Pablo quickly whispered, "Don't forget, we've got the spirit of Jim."

Rose was invited to join them up front, then Pastor Reed opened the service with hymns. To show his efforts toward equality, he offered to have Rose lead the time prayers. Colton felt out of place facing the congregation, but Rose led the congregation with beautiful prayers. At long last, the pastor turned the service over to Pablo. Colton was still nervous, but Pablo spoke eloquently and with conviction about Jim Caldwell. They were surprised when church folk became believers, so they remained for a long time afterwards and Pablo and Rose both spoke boldly for the Lord. As the time grew from one to two to three hours, Pablo began doing signs and wonders of healing and imparting hope. Things were going great for the missioners, but not for long.

Word got around the city over the next several days about the stories of Jim Caldwell, and the residents became divided. Some believed the stories while others thought Pablo, Rose, and Colton to be charlatans. As is so often common, the troublemakers won out, and began breathing threats against them. Pastor Reed hurried to their boarding house, and with apologies, suggested they leave town. All of a sudden they sensed their work was done, so Pablo, Colton, and Rose packed their things and headed for the train station. As usual, Colton asked, "Where to next?"

Truth is, Pablo wanted to go to Albuquerque, but the ticket person started explaining all kinds of problems with the railroads not wanting to work together. The man droned on about the Denver and Rio Grande Western Railroad and their agreement problems with the Atchison, Topeka and Santa Fe Railroad. Pablo really wasn't interested in a history lesson, so he finally interrupted and said, "I'll take three tickets to Santa Fe." He was frustrated that they couldn't get him all the way to Albuquerque, but he knew it would all work out. After they disembarked at Sant Fe, they bought three horses with the extra money they still had, and then completed their trip to Albuquerque.

---

The first thing Pablo announced was that he was kind of done with speaking in churches, so they spent some time riding around Albuquerque. The Spirit of Jim was certainly not confined within the walls of a church, so they hoped for some new good fortune with street preaching. Pablo was just soaking up the culture, because the town was a distant outpost of the Spanish empire, and its residents were mostly people who looked like himself. It was also the site of Native American pueblos when Europeans first arrived in 1540, and was officially founded in 1706 by Don Francisco Cuervo y Valdés. It soon became an important trading center on the Chihuahua Trail from Mexico.

That's when Pablo saw his first opportunity to do his

# The Value of the Diamond

missionary work in Albuquerque. He stopped, and motioned to Colton and Rose to dismount. They walked up to a man sitting by the street, and soon discovered he had been crippled from birth. Pablo started sharing his story with the man, when he sensed the man had faith to be healed. Speaking in a loud voice, Pablo said, "Stand upright on your feet." Crowds had already gathered when the man sprang up and began to walk. They all knew the man who had been healed, so they shouted, "¡Los dioses han llegado a nosotras en forma humana!" which means "The gods have come down to us in human form!"

To their surprise, the crowds rushed away. It turned out that there was a local shaman just outside town who listened to the story that excited the crowd. It didn't take him long to suggest they offer sacrifices to Pablo and Colton for their great gift. The people headed off in different directions to find the best gifts they could gather. Returning to Pablo and Colton, they brought turquoise and silver jewelry, and a very rare Yawanawá necklace made in Brazil, and some onyx figurines from Mexico.

Pablo was touched, but knew that the praise was going the wrong direction. He finally said, "Friends, why are you doing this? We are mortals just like you, and we bring you good news, that you should turn from these worthless things to the living God, who made the heaven and the earth and the sea and all that is in them. In past generations he allowed all the nations to follow their own ways; yet he has not left himself without a witness in doing good—giving you rains from heaven and fruitful seasons, and filling you with food and your hearts with joy."

But the crowds did not listen. In fact, they were downright incensed. They felt Pablo was unappreciative of their gifts, and one person questioned, "Did he just call our gifts worthless?"

# The Value of the Diamond

The crowd was quickly turning angry, as another said, "You are not a god, we now agree with you, for gods would not turn down such precious gifts" At that point things turned very ugly for the visitors, and Pablo and Colton were severely beaten. They were dragged out of town and left for dead, but they decided to leave Rose alone. She got some water, tended to their wounds, and after several hours, they woke up. They were bloodied and in severe pain, as Rose asked, "Pablo, Colton. You alive?" Pablo weakly responded, "I think so," and Colton nodded his head yes.

They laid there for a while, taking inventory of their injuries, and were glad to find they had no broken bones. When Rose finally managed to drag them to their feet and lean them against their horses, Pablo curled a smile that their horses were also loyal. The horses had stayed nearby, and were more ready for the remaining trip than their riders. Rose first tried to push Pablo up on his horse. He was facing his horse in a standing position as Rose firmly placed her hand on his buttocks. She said, "If this isn't ministry, I don't know what is!" but nobody had the energy to laugh. With one big shove, Pablo sprawled over the saddle. He slowly turned over, with lots of help from Rose, and many moans and groans. Likewise, Rose helped him move one leg over the saddle and he carefully sat up.

"Next!" exclaimed a joyful Rose, but Colton had no joy. She said, "Oh, come on. At least I learned some things from getting Pablo on his horse." Working together, Colton got on his colt and readied himself, then Rose mounted her steed. Even though they were bloodied and had torn clothes, Colton managed to ask, "Where to now?" Pablo said, "I think we've done enough here." They both laughed through the pain and all three headed back to the church in Flagstaff.

# The Value of the Diamond

It was more than a 300 mile journey ahead of them, and the first several miles were just grueling. As time passed by, so did some of their pain. They slowly learned how to sit in the saddle in less difficult ways, but they still wanted to stop. Pablo suggested it would be too hard to get on and off again, so they rode until dusk. It was cool in the mountains, so when the sun set, they picked a campsite, got off their horses, and Rose prepared a fire. It reminded Pablo of their first night by the Grand Canyon, and he wondered how Kate was doing. Missing her robust attitude and amazing testimony, he drifted off to sleep.

Each day was a challenge, but at least they knew they were always getting closer. Wounds were slowly healing and so was their spirit, and it really helped having Rose with them. She did a great job of keeping them positive. Crossing the Puerco River was a celebration of its own, as they knew it meant they were back in the Arizona Territory. They followed the Purerco River and passed some magnificent scenery. They saw fallen trees that looked like colorful stone, and Colton hoped that someday the area would be preserved.

The next day they passed through a small, unincorporated town. They were standing on a corner in Winslow, Arizona and thought the small General Store was such a fine sight to see. They went in and got some cheese, hardtack, coffee, and dried fruit, and praised God for the opportunity to get some supplies. That lasted them all the way home, but when they arrived, the Caldwellians were appalled at their appearance. They helped them dismount, assisted them into the church, and told them to get some rest.

The next morning, the church gathered together to hear all that happened on their missionary journey. First they

# The Value of the Diamond

celebrated having come full circle in their travels through the American West, then explained Kate's absence. Most of the Caldwellians were wide-eyed at their accounts of troubles in Salt Lake City, Denver, and Albuquerque, and decided then and there that mission work was not for them. Pablo was feeling a bit defensive, so he shared the good experiences they had on their journeys and was a bit surprised when the stories finished so fast. Pablo ended by saying, "Well, at least a door has been opened for faith in Jim Caldwell. Sometimes you just plant the seeds of faith and let others reap the harvest." And they stayed in Flagstaff with the Caldwellian church members for some time.

# The Value of the Diamond

## SCENE TWO
### Mexico City and Guadalajara

**W**hile in Flagstaff, Pablo got a telegram from Mexico City. His experiences, both in Mexico and North America, helped him answer the concerns expressed by the Caldwellian Church.

---

HOLA PABLO,

REMIND US OF THE KEY POINTS OF THE FAITH.
REMIND US HOW TO LIVE THAT FAITH.

APPRECIATIVELY,
THE CALDWELLIANS OF MEXICO CITY

---

Remembering the troubles he had in that city, he lightly chuckled as he addressed them as "saints." Knowing the seriousness of his task, he proceeded with "Grace to you and peace from God our Father and the Lord Jim Caldwell." Now that this was his third response to a telegram, he decided to again refer to Jim as Lord, like he did when writing to the Nogalesites. He knew 'Lord' was the term used to refer to the deified Russian emperor, and that was precisely his point. Not only was it a political and religious statement, it followed the revolutionary thinking of Jim Caldwell. Jim was greater than any human idol, because the resurrection was what set him apart.

# The Value of the Diamond

Well, not just resurrection. Jim had innumerable redeeming qualities, and just thinking about them again brought joy to Pablo's heart. He still struggled to understand why, of all people, Jim chose him to "know" about the resurrection. For whatever reason though, he was certainly dedicating the rest of his life to sharing that profound good news.

Pablo then scribbled some initial ideas for an opening prayer in his letter to them. He had heard that prayer was extremely important to the historical Jim, so he started with a beatitude. Pablo felt particularly good as he exhorted the Capitalinos to be "holy and blameless before him in love." The next words he jotted down were redemption and forgiveness, then he made sure to use the word mystery, since it seemed so relevant to his own experience. Then he thought that he certainly needed to include the word hope. He learned a lot about hope as he sat in jail for three years feeling hopeless. He put his pen down and thought and prayed about his responses as he sat in his room in the modest church home.

After a while, he wrote that he was remembering them in his prayers, and specifically prayed that they would receive a spirit of wisdom. He knew the problems the Capitalinos faced with living in a city near such a magnificent place as Teotihuacan. It is just thirty miles northeast of Mexico City and consisted of the Pyramid of the Sun and the Pyramid of the Moon, connected by the Avenue of the Dead. The problem was that the locals made miniature souvenirs of the pyramids for visitors from all over the world, which made the business one of near idolatry. It was almost a carnival atmosphere, which seemed exceedingly strange and frustrating to Pablo because the ancient Aztecs considered it a sacred place. It reminded him of the time he stood at the Grand Canyon, which made him hope even more that tourism wouldn't some day ruin it's majesty. This all seemed too depressing, so Pablo decided to go outside and get some fresh air.

It was a crisp and cool day in the mountains of northern Arizona. The birds were chirping and squirrels were running around the yard, and Pablo couldn't quite put his finger on the joy he felt. It crossed his mind that there seemed to be a spiritual connection between everything. That was just what his spirit needed to continue with this important letter, so he sat outside on the front porch. He penned his hope that this wisdom would enlighten their hearts, so that they might know God's will for them. He noted that God put his power to work when he raised Jim from the dead, and suggested that Jim would take a seat of honor in heaven.

Pablo wanted to finish this opening prayer saying something new, or at least since his letter to the Nogalesites. After thinking for a moment, he smiled because it came to him that his inspiration while being in the out-of-doors was starting to materialize. The interconnectedness of life slowly became visualized in a strange way. Pablo saw Jim's head on top of a church. It wasn't a disembodied image, but a connected one. Jim may no longer be with them physically, so why not have them think of the church as his body? This concept would now let Jim be the head over all things for the Caldwellian churches.

He then stopped for a moment to remind himself about the first concern in the telegram. He glanced at it and remembered that they wanted to know the key points of the faith. Pablo decided to begin by talking about life without God, then compare it to life with God. He was pleased with how he was going to begin the body of his letter, but first he needed another break to really get in touch with Jim's spirit. Pablo walked down to a local café to get some coffee, and immediately thought about The Rusty Tavern back in Phoenix. He sat outside and sipped his drink, and soaked up some sun, then it hit him. Thoughts of his old life just flooded back, and even he was surprised about the dramatic change it was to the new life in Jim.

As he hurried back to his room's porch to continue his letter, he wondered where Timoteo might be. He proved to be a great ambassador for Jim, and did a wonderful job carrying Pablo's letters to the Nogalesites and Chihuahuans. But now he was on his own, evangelizing in the name of Jim Caldwell, so Pablo wasn't sure what he would do to get this letter to the people of Mexico City. When he got back to his room, he again prepared to put pen to paper. So, life without God, eh? Pablo started writing furiously about how sin causes one to live as if they were dead. He warned that a Godless life fills the soul with the desires of the flesh, leaving us as children of wrath, like everyone else.

Pablo paused again, realizing that just thinking about his old life was turning his soul dark. He felt his chest tighten as he thought about dragging Caldwellians to Marshal Garfias, so he proceeded with thoughts about God being rich in mercy. Tears started to fall as he penned "by grace you have been saved." His mind wandered back for a moment to his road to Tucson experience and a smile crept across his face. Knowing how undeserving he was, Pablo continued with "For by grace you have been saved through faith, and this is not your own doing; it is the gift of God—not the result of works, so that no one may boast." He then wrote about being created anew in Jim Caldwell, and that it should be our new way of life.

The old life, Pablo explained, was the life without the spirit of Jim. It was a lonely life, not knowing promise nor God. But now in Jim Caldwell, we are brought together. We have peace, because there is no need for hostility, not even towards those who wrong us. There is no dividing wall, because one humanity can be created in the name of Jim. He continued writing with, "So then we are no longer strangers and sojourners, but members of the household of God. And we are joined together spiritually, into the Caldwellian Church that is open to all. When I say all, I mean all. That is, it does not matter where we came from, or what we look like, or what we have done. God loves us and is interested in who we are now and where we are going. When the community comes together in such a loving way, we become a dwelling place for God."

Pablo stopped again, and was pleased. He felt inspired about what he had written, and prayed about what else God wanted him to tell the Capitalinos. Immediately he sensed the spirit of Jim leading him to talk about the mystery of God's plan. It was time to tell them that all people were chosen by God, and that the Caldwellian Church was to make God's wisdom known. What better way to show inclusion than to tell his own story, so he shared quickly about his unique revelation from the risen Lord. Pablo was excited to share that this great mystery had never before been revealed, but now it was theirs to know: anyone can share in the promise of Jim Caldwell, through the good news of his resurrection.

Pablo concluded this part of his letter with prayers for the Caldwellian Capitalinos. He wanted them to be strengthened in their inner being, because he knew that spreading the news of God's love through Jim would be a challenge. He then wrote something about how he sincerely prayed for them to have spiritual power, and that they needed to have Jim's spirit dwelling in their heart. The reason was because he knew that having Jim's spirit within would ground them in love. Then he prayed that they might be able to comprehend the breadth and length and height and depth of God's work. He liked that. It seemed to express the fullness of their task. Finally, he desired that they would be able to know the love of Jim which passes all understanding.

Satisfied, Pablo looked back again at the telegram. A smile crept across his face, because he was glad they wanted to know how to put their faith into practice. Theory, he thought to himself, was virtually worthless if you don't do anything about it. He begged them to live a worthwhile and meaningful life, because the meaning of life is to live a life of meaning. The way to do that is to be humble and gentle and patient. Pablo was on a roll now, and the words just flowed. "There is one body and one Spirit, just as you were called to the one hope of your calling, one Lord, one faith, one baptism."

He then explained that we were given grace according to the measure of Jim's gift. Again the inspiration just flowed with, "The gifts he gave were that some would be vaqueros, some caballeros, some evangelisticos, some padres, and some maestras." He encouraged them to find their gifts, so they would mature to the measure and stature of the fullness of Jim. Pablo then exhorted them to speak the truth in love, for the purpose of building the community in love. He further insisted that they put away their former life, and be renewed in their mind. That way they would be clothed with the new life.

Pablo couldn't help but think something needed to be written about the things that destroy Caldwellian community, so he encouraged them to put away falsehood. Especially because Caldwellians were accused of spreading fake news, he demanded that they exorcise gossip from their lives. He knew that would be an endless challenge, so he told them to treat it like an evil addiction. He knew first hand about the damage gossip could do. The whole reason he spent three years in prison in Mexico City was because the 'policia' listened to the gossip that said resurrection was fake news. All of a sudden he felt hot all over with anger, and decided to address that issue.

He explained that it was okay to be angry, but not to sin, because anger is just a feeling, while sin is what we do with it. He then decided to give them something to think about: "all sin is wrong doing, but not all wrong doing is sin." He hoped they would dwell on that long enough to understand it. Further, he was emphatic that they must put away all hatred that dwells in the heart. Instead, they needed to be the first to be forgiving, because God showed the way by forgiving us through the death of his son Jim. Finally, he encouraged them to be imitators of God, to live in love, because Jim first loved us and gave himself up for us.

Something kept bothering Pablo about the old life everyone has, before they turn to the new life of Jim. He suggested that fornication and impurity should not even be mentioned, then implored them to act in the ways of Jim. He warned them that obscene, silly, and vulgar talk was entirely out of place in the community, then plainly said that no one should be deceptive. To really make his point, he wrote that they should not even associate with those who do, then he realized one of Jim's first followers was Big Nose Kate who had been a prostitute. And Matt had run a house of prostitution. "Oh well," he thought. "I guess that's part of why this whole thing is called a mystery." Then he decided that you can't judge a book by what's on the outside.

He also realized that the Capitalinos needed practical advice, and it needed to be simple and straightforward. So he wrote that the old life was darkness, but the new life is light, so take no part in darkness, but shine light on it. He explained that the days are evil, so it is of utmost importance to understand God's will. Don't get drunk on spirits, but be filled with the Spirit. He wrote that they should, "Sing psalms and hymns, making melody to the Lord in your hearts." Then he wrote that they should give thanks to God at all times and for everything in the name of our Lord Jim Caldwell.

Pablo paused again to refresh and spend some time in prayer. He felt certain that he was being properly inspired, but wasn't sure where to go next with his letter. After a quick nap, he decided to share some of those thoughts he had when he started, about the church being Jim's body. The words began to flow, so he wrote "Submit to one another out of reverence for Jim." He hoped the readers wouldn't misunderstand, because his point was about equality. He continued about having Jim as the head of the church in community as well as in the family, and this is put to use in love. If the spirit of Jim loves the church, then the spirit of Jim loves the family, and we are all one: Jim, church, and family. Pablo then scribbled another note about making it all very practical through respect.

About that time, a young family went walking by. The baby in the stroller was doing fine, but the child walking next to the stroller was very loud and angry. Pablo couldn't believe that neither parent did anything while the child was screaming and throwing a fit. Pablo thanked God for this useful interruption, and began writing about family. "Children, obey your parents." That didn't seem too confusing, so he bolstered this statement with scripture: "Honor your father and mother." Figuring that many readers wouldn't know scripture, he explained that Exodus 20:12 contained a promise. For those who obey this commandment, they should be able to live long in the land where they dwell. He then warned parents to not provoke their children to anger. Having no children, Pablo felt that was enough to say about that.

He was ready to close out his letter, but something kept nudging him to give the Capitalinos an image of protection. All he could think about was the cowboy clothes he heard that Jim wore. Before he knew it, he was writing about being strong in the Lord and in the strength of his power. He penned that they should put on the whole cowboy outfit of Jim, so they could stand against evil. This inspired Pablo to remind them that their struggle was against the rulers and authorities and cosmic powers of this present darkness. Now Pablo felt he needed to be bold, so he turned his image of Jim's cowboy outfit into the Mexican cowboy clothes of the vaqueros.

To fight spiritual evil, he pleaded with them to stand firm in the whole outfit of God's protection. He wrote that they should "put on the sombrero of salvation, so it covers your head like the waters of baptism. Wrap yourself in the bolero of righteousness, and wear it as a reminder of the good works you are called to do. Toss the serape of faith over your shoulders, and let the fringe at the bottom drip troubles away. Climb into the chaps of truth, so you are bolstered with God's way. Slide your feet into the botas of peace, so that you can walk this life like Jim Crawford did. Finally, strap on the spurs of God's word, and use them as the machete of the Spirit."

Pablo felt great about that piece of inspiration. He followed it with a request for himself, that he would be given a boldness when he spoke of the mystery of the gospel. He then let them know he would be sending Diego, who could tell them everything about his situation. He explained that Diego was a dear brother he met among the Caldwellians of Flagstaff, and that he was a faithful minister in the name of Jim Caldwell. Diego's main purpose was to encourage their hearts in the exciting and challenging task of living as a Caldwellian.

He then closed his letter with a benediction. Pablo wished them peace and love and faith, from God the Father and the Lord Jim Caldwell. Something frustrating entered his mind at that moment, and for some reason he couldn't bring himself to offer blessings to those who didn't have an undying love for Jim. He felt it wasn't right, but a little impish grin came across his face when he thought of a subtle way to hold back blessings.

He picked up his pen and wrote his last sentence: "Grace be with all who have an undying love for our Lord Jim Crawford."

He then put his letter in an envelope and sealed it. He gathered the church members together to lay their hands on Diego's head for a blessing, and said, "Dear God our Father and Jim our Lord, we pray safety for Diego's journey. He has many miles to travel on several kinds of passage. Give him rest and nourishment all the way to Mexico City. We are thankful for his boldness to accept such a great challenge, and pray he may arrive with health in his mind, body, and soul. Be with him as he turns this letter over to our dear brothers and sisters in that great capital city." Diego then mounted his horse and rode off for an initial stop in Phoenix. A member of the church said, "If that letter makes it all the way to Mexico City, it could only be by the grace of God."

Pablo was pleased how the Caldwellian church was growing all over North America. He got word from Phoenix that church structure was settling in and the word about Jim was still growing with great speed. He also rejoiced that his work with the people in Mexico was having wonderful success. He thought about Pedro's work with the people in the United States, and quickly moved on to a more enjoyable topic. He stopped for a moment, and wondered why he was so willing to not think about Pedro, and it bothered him deeply. Then again this was a struggle about authority, and Pablo realized he was still frustrated about how Pedro treated him as inferior. Pedro insisted that his direct experience with Jim during his earthly ministry was far superior to Pablo's direct experience with Jim from heaven.

The fury that built up inside him came quickly and was unholy, and he even began questioning his calling to spread the news about Jim. Pablo wondered why he couldn't let this issue go about Pedro disrespecting him, and he felt remorse for a moment, then a light bulb went on. Even though he was imperfect in so many ways, God still used him to write letters to help others. It was one of those moments that changes things. Or could have. He quickly got back to thinking about Pedro's faults. With some false bravado, Pablo hoped that some day Pedro would realize that the church was about living like Jim did when he was on earth. He started focusing on how wrong Pedro was, and that his problem was that he needed to be led today by the Spirit of Jim from heaven. Both parts are essential to the Caldwellian life. He decided the sad thing was that Pedro was actually envious of him for having his transforming experience, but because they never talked honestly with each other, the problem never got resolved.

———

# The Value of the Diamond

Toward the end of Pablo's stay in Flagstaff, he got another telegram. He enjoyed hearing from churches in Mexico that wanted his help, because it inflated his ego. This helped deter his anger about the unhealed 'thorn' in his flesh, which now just might be more about Pedro. It was good to know the churches that he founded, and the ones that were already there, were surviving. Times were certainly difficult in the United States and Mexico, but life was changing rapidly. Pablo just prayed that the spirit of Jim would continue to find open souls, so they could be led in a holy way. He opened the letter and found it was from the good people at the church of Guadalajara. Pablo fondly recalled the people there, and loved the city that he considered to be the quintessential representation of Mexico. Here's what was on the telegram:

ESTIMADO PABLO,

YOU ARE IN JAIL? WE'RE CONCERNED!
WE ARE ALSO CONCERNED THAT SOME
    AMERICAN MISSIONARIES ARE PREACHING A
    DIFFERENT GOSPEL THAN YOURS.
AND WE ARE HAVING TROUBLE WITH OUR
    LEADERSHIP.

ATENTAMENTE,
THE CALDWELLIAN CHURCH OF GUADALAJARA

As Pablo read over the concerns, he welled up with anger inside. He wondered "Why would missionaries change the message? How dare they!" And when he read about problems with the leadership, his soul burned hot. As he sat in his room, he had plenty of time to settle down. He needed a clear head before he replied, so he rested, then prayed, and then started writing, even though he was disappointed that he let his old self slip out.

"To all the saints in Guadalajara, and the overseers and helpers; grace to you and peace, in the name of Jim Caldwell."

That felt pretty good. He again loved the implication that the overseers and helpers were not part of the saints. After all, they were part of the problem. He continued by sharing his thankfulness for the Guadalajran believers, and that he prayed for them all the time. He wrote about his confidence that everything would be okay, either in this life or the next. Pablo was strangely moved as he wrote, "For God as my witness; how I long for all of you with the compassion of Jim." He genuinely meant it, even though his heart was filled with anger about the situation. He then talked about his hope for their growth in knowledge and insight.

As for his being in jail, he explained that he was released after three years in Mexico City, and is now in the United States. He then wrote, "I want you to know that what has happened to me has actually helped to spread the gospel. It has become known to everyone here that my imprisonment was for our Lord Jim Caldwell. Not only that, but the new believers are daring to speak with greater boldness and without fear." He went on to say that some were making fun of the story of Jim, but others were proclaiming Jim out of love. He then asked, "What does it matter? Just this, that Jim is proclaimed in every way, whether out of false motives or true; and in that I rejoice."

Pablo urged them to believe that he would always be delivered from a prison, because his salvation would deliver him to the next life, even if he didn't get out of jail in this life. Then he wrote, "It is my eager expectation and hope that I will not be put to shame in any way, so I need to speak the truth. Jim will be exalted now as always, whether by life or by death." He tried to explain that, at least for himself, living was about Jim, and dying was even better, but he realized this could be taken wrong. That's when he added that it was more necessary for them to live for the sake of glorifying and sharing about Jim. After all, Pablo wasn't ready to die either. He had demons of his own he was still fighting, and hoped that doing good for the rest of his life would keep him on the straight and narrow.

He decided he needed to shift his focus to the wonderful people of Guadalajara. Pablo stopped again and waited for some inspiration, which came with surprising ease and speed. He proceeded to tell them to live a life worthy of the gospel. He exhorted them to stand firm in the guidance of the spirit of Jim, and to strive together with one mind for the faith of the gospel, so they can keep from being intimidated by their opponents. He told them to know, without doubt, that if they accomplish difficult tasks, they can celebrate that it was God working with them. Then he told them a great secret: "For he has graciously granted you the privilege not only of believing in Jim, but of suffering for him as well—since you are having the same struggle that you heard I had."

Pablo felt a need to offer more encouragement, since suffering isn't very appealing, so he wrote, "If there is any consolation from love, any sharing in the Spirit, any compassion and sympathy, make my joy complete: be of the same mind, having the same love, being in full accord and of one mind." He felt this was so important, he offered the following advice on how to keep it from happening. He told them to not be selfish or conceited, but regard others as better than yourselves. He begged them to put the needs of others as a primary concern, because that would give them the same mind as Jim Caldwell.

All of this inspiration was doing something to Pablo. He didn't fully understand it, but he decided to write it down. The words strangely fell from his pen and he wrote the words in a creative fashion, unlike he'd ever done. To him it felt like poetry, but when he was done writing, he realized it was about the story of Jim's life:

Let the same mind be in you
that was in Jim Caldwell,
who was a child of God,
just like you and me,
but he took the form of a cowboy,
being born a human.
And being in human form,
he humbled himself
and became obedient to the point of death—
even death by a rope.

Therefore God also highly exalted him
when he arrived in heaven,
and gave him the name
that is above every name,
so that at the name of Jim
every knee should bend,

in heaven and on earth,
and every tongue should confess
that Jim Caldwell is Lord,
to the glory of God the Father.

# The Value of the Diamond

Pablo reread what he wrote, and thought that someday it might become a song. But however it might be used in the future, he prayed that it would show the way of humility and obedience. He hoped they would catch the significance of humiliation being replaced with exaltation. Pablo then complemented them for their obedience, not only when he was present with them but also when he was absent. He also suggested that the more they worked together for good, the more they could fend off the outside troublemakers.

Again he stopped, and this time he thought about God's children complaining in the wilderness, so he wrote, "Do all things without murmuring and arguing, so that you may be blameless and innocent, children of God without blemish in the midst of a crooked and perverse generation, in which you shine like stars in the world." He wasn't sure that even he believed that, but it should provide impetus for their proper behavior. He further suggested that sacrifice was something they should rejoice in, for it was the way of Jim.

He stopped for a moment, looked back at the telegram, and got angry reading about missionaries preaching a different gospel. Actually, he was so angry that he expressed it in his letter, writing that they should beware of the low life dogs who are evil missionaries. Pablo knew he had to cool down, so he waited for a while and prayed about it. Soon he was back to writing, only this time it was in a positive light. He explained that nothing was more important than knowing the spirit of Jim, and that comes through faith. Pablo had to be careful here, because Pedro and The Twelve actually knew the earthly Jim. He had to make sure the Capitalinos understood his road to Tucson experience was so powerful, that their faith in the risen Lord would also be as good as Pedro's historical experience.

# The Value of the Diamond

Pablo thought that maybe he needed to correct himself. He wrote that he was certainly not perfect, but he was on the road to being complete, and that is only because Jim Caldwell brought him into the family of believers. Then the words just flowed. He wrote, "this one thing I do: forgetting what lies behind and straining forward to what lies ahead, I press on toward the goal for the prize of the upward call of God in the name of Jim Caldwell. Let those of us then who are mature be of the same mind; and if you think differently about anything, this too God will reveal to you. Only let us hold fast to the gospel message given from God, through Jim, to me, and shared properly with you."

He got frustrated again about the improper message the missionaries were sharing with them. In fact, he got so mad that he wadded up the letter and threw it into the trash can. He took a break to cool down, which was frustratingly often. Getting new writing paper, he again put pen to paper, but the anger just wouldn't go away. "For many live as enemies of Jim; I have often told you of them, and now I tell you even with tears. Their end is destruction; their god is the belly; and their glory is in their shame; their minds are set on earthly things." Pablo reminded them that they are citizens of God's Kingdom here on earth, which will lead them to becoming citizens of God's Kingdom in heaven. He finished his thought by telling them that they were his beloved church, and that they were his joy and crown. He felt very two-faced about all of this, but knew that it wasn't easy to practice what you preach.

That being done, he looked back at the telegram, and saw that they were also having troubles within their leadership. "Will the maddening problems never stop?" he wondered. Pablo decided to name two women he knew, and urged them to stop causing trouble. He then asked a special friend in the church to help the two women. He felt divine revelation seeping into his heart, which he desperately needed, then wrote, "Rejoice in the Lord always; again I will say, Rejoice." Pablo then wrote that they should spend much time in prayer, thanking God for the precious gift of life. He explained that the peace of God surpasses all understanding, but it would guide their hearts and minds in the name of Jim.

Pablo knew he had to close out his letter on a positive note. After all, being a messenger of good news does not mean ignoring the bad news, it just means that the good news is what we Caldwellians choose to do. He wrote that "whatever is honorable, whatever is just, whatever is pure, whatever is pleasing, whatever is commendable, if there is any excellence and if there is anything worthy of praise, think about these things." Pablo wished he could do that, then got back to his favorite topic, celebrating their concern for him. Again he felt Jim's spirit nudging him in his writing, so he penned "I know what it is to have little, and I know what it is to have plenty. In any and all circumstances I have learned the secret of being well-fed and of going hungry, of having plenty and of being in need. I can do all things though Jim who strengthens me."

Pablo sat back and thought about that last piece, and agreed with it. His mind went back to the time he persecuted the Caldwellians and he felt a twinge of shame. Then he realized that without his background, he would be in no need of his road to Tucson experience. Yes, coming to know the spirit of Jim was what faith was all about, and anyone could have that experience. Pablo was content for now, which was needed because he was going to talk to them about money. He knew that was a delicate issue, so he had to proceed carefully to keep from being misunderstood.

He reminded the Guadalajarans that they were the only Caldwellian church that helped in the early days. And he was especially grateful that when he was beginning his Mexican work in Nogales, they even sent help for his needs more than once. Then he acknowledged the current gifts they sent, and called them "a fragrant offering, a sacrifice acceptable and pleasing to God." He said that God would satisfy their needs too, and give the glory to God. He finished by telling them to greet every saint in the name of Jim Caldwell, and bid them the grace of Jim to be with their spirit, then closed with "amen."

Another departure was arranged by the Caldwellian community of Flagstaff. They were called upon to equip Timoteo and Eduardo who had been chosen for this journey to Guadalajara. They needed horses to get to Nogales, then a train to Guadalajara. It wasn't as far as Diego had to go to deliver Pablo's letter to the people of Mexico City, but it was still a monumental trip. Pablo called everyone together and they formed a circle. He put Timoteo and Eduardo in the middle of the circle, then had everyone move in close and put their hands on either their head or their shoulders. Pablo put his hands on each of the heads, then prayed over the men and the letter, and sent them off with requests for divine protection.

## ACT III
### FAMILIARITY BREEDS CONTEMPT

Mexico, Mid 1890's

# The Value of the Diamond

## SCENE ONE
Teotihuacan

Pablo and Colton and Rose were appalled to hear that, even in the U.S., there were missionaries and evangelists who were demanding that the Caldwellians follow the law that was given to Abund. Pablo stood wide-eyed as he listened to heretical stories claiming that without the Law you cannot be saved. Pablo quickly called a meeting with the church in Flagstaff, and they decided to send Pablo, Colton and Rose to Phoenix to discuss this insidious problem with the mother church. They were informed that the church was getting organized, and now even had elders. Pablo rolled his eyes and said, "Sure wish the church was more about serving others than helping themselves!"

When they got to Phoenix, they were warmly welcomed. They settled into the new church the Caldwellians were working from and shared many stories about their travels through Mexico and America, with all of its ups and downs. They delighted in recalling the memories of people coming to Jim's abundant life by way of faith, and the four letters he had written in response to telegrams from churches. To Pablo's surprise, one of the elders stood up and said, "It is necessary to keep the law of Abund. Without them, there is no salvation!" It was all Pablo could do to restrain himself as his face grew hot with anger again. He felt like grabbing someone's riding crop and giving the man a good horse-whipping.

Instead, the mother church decided to call together its leadership to discuss the matter. The next day, the small group of decision makers gathered around a table. As usual, they left one chair empty to symbolize Jim Caldwell's presence. Pablo watched with curiosity, because he was very surprised to see that Johnny, one of the original twelve, had taken over the position of leader. Pablo was not one to keep quiet, but this development kept him on the sidelines. At least for a while.

Soon enough, Pedro spoke up. (You remember Pedro, Pablo's nemesis?) He stood up and reminded them about the Holy Spirit falling on unbelievers during his visit with Hank in Wickenburg. He said, "In the early days, God made a choice among you, that I should be the one through whom the unbelievers would hear the message of the good news and become believers. And God, who knows the human heart, testified to them by giving them the Holy Spirit, just as he did to us; and in cleansing their hearts by faith he has made no distinction between them and us." Then Pedro yelled, "Now therefore why are you putting God to the test? We believe that we will be saved through the grace of the Lord Jim, just as they will. Enough with this talk of needing the law!"

The church was silenced by Pedro's speech, so Pablo, Colton, and Rose began sharing their stories with the leaders, after explaining about Kate's departure. For one fleeting moment, there was a sense that Pedro and Pablo were working together. The leaders of the mother church were amazed that Pablo and Colton got to the famous Havasu Falls, and were overjoyed to hear the Shaman agreed to be baptized. They were astounded that Pablo, Colton, and Rose traveled by horseback all the way to Salt Lake City, and they were stunned to hear that Pablo spoke at an LDS Church. After hearing that the sermon was well received, they were not surprised to hear that angry mobs later that week ran them out of town. The elders were pleased to hear that they chose to take a train, and could barely believe Pablo decided to head next to Denver. Pablo had to remind them it was the leadership of the spirit of Jim.

The apostles and elders continued to listen, as Pablo shared his story about Pastor Ross inviting him to preach at his First Congregational Church. Pablo told about doing signs and wonders in their midst, how the townspeople became divided, and how Pastor Ross encouraged them to leave while they could. Colton then talked about their experience in Albuquerque, and how Pablo healed a man crippled from birth. The elders applauded, until Colton told them the crowd thought Pablo was a god. Rose said that when they brought gifts to Pablo, he turned them down, but the crowd was offended. "What happened?" inquired Johnny, to which Colton said, "We were nearly beaten to death." All of a sudden, several elders decided missionary work wasn't for them.

Rose shared about their excruciating journey back to Flagstaff and the letters Pablo wrote in response to telegrams form churches he started. Pablo continued with stories about his journey to Mexico, and after he finished talking, Johnny said, "Listen to me. Pedro has told us how God first looked favorably on the unbelievers." Pablo was visibly upset, because he was thinking that it seemed like a waste of time that he ever bothered to share his stories. Then Johnny continued, "This agrees with the words of the prophets, as it is written,

'After this I will return,
    and I will rebuild the dwelling of Montezuma,
        which has fallen;
    from its ruins I will rebuild it,
        and I will set it up,

so that all other peoples may seek the Lord—
even all the unbelievers over whom my name has
been called.

Thus says the Lord, who has been making these
things known from long ago.'

In light of these reports, I have reached the decision that we should not trouble those unbelievers who are turning to God, but we should write to them to abstain from idols and from fornication."

Pablo thought this was all a bit unnecessary, because he himself had direct guidance from the spirit of Jim, but then he calmed down and decided to cooperate with this newfangled church administration. The elders decided to send Pablo, Rose, and Colton back to Flagstaff with a letter. Pablo was a bit surprised, but glad to hear they were moving in the right direction. Here's what the letter said, as signed by Johnny.

"Greetings to the converted brothers and sisters of Flagstaff. Since we have heard that certain persons who have gone out from us, though with no instructions from us, have said things to disturb you and have unsettled your minds, we have unanimously decided to send back to you Colton and Pablo, and Rose, who have risked their lives for the sake of our Lord Jim Caldwell. For it has seemed good to the Holy Spirit and to us to impose on you no further burden than these essentials: that you abstain from idols, and from fornication. If you keep yourselves from these, you will do well. Farewell."

So they mounted their horses and headed off to Flagstaff. Pablo enjoyed passing familiar sights, like the Rusty Tavern and the road to Jerome, even though things were changing around them quickly. When they got to Flagstaff, they gathered the faithful together and gave them the letter. When they read it, they were happy, so Rose, Pablo and Colton remained in Flagstaff to teach and preach the word about Jim. After some days Pablo said to Colton, "I want to return to Mexico to see how the churches I started are doing." Colton was open to the possibility, but demanded a new friend of his come along. Pablo wasn't used to demands, so the friendly discussion quickly became an argument. In fact, it became so intense that they parted company. Colton headed north with his new friend to the places that had been visited in the United States, and Pablo ended up selecting an exciting new recruit from the Caldwellian Church in Flagstaff named Jasper. Together they headed south to Mexico, along with Rose.

---

The three of them took the train to Guadalajara, the capitol of the Mexican state of Jalisco, because it was more than 1,300 miles away. They caught the train at Nogales, Arizona, and Pablo was disappointed with himself for not crossing the border and visiting the Caldwellians in Nogales, Mexico. When they finally arrived in Guadalajara, they were mesmerized by the size and beauty of the city. Acting like tourists, they visited the city center, which was dotted with colonial plazas and landmarks. They were in awe of the neoclassical Teatro Degollado, then took a seat in the central plaza. Soon a mariachi band stopped at their table and a waitress took their order. Seeing how tequila was born there, they ordered a margarita. Jasper felt strange about ordering alcohol, but Pablo settled him down by saying, "When in Guadalajara, do as the Guadalajarans do." Rose stunned them by ordering a Vino Mezcal de Tequila de Jose Cuervo. Noticing their faces, she said, "Hey guys, remember, I'm not Kate."

After spending several days in the city, they wanted a calmer atmosphere, so they headed to the outskirts of town. Since it was the Sabbath, they were delighted to find a peaceful spot by the Rio Grande de Santiago River, where there was also a small group of women gathering stones for their craft. They sat down by the women, and Pablo began sharing his gospel message. They were very hesitant, as they were suspicious of men, not to mention "Americanos".

One of the women was named Guadalupe. She was from Aguascalientes, a worshiper of God, and a maker of fine jewelry. As she listened, the others continued to ignore him, because they also didn't understand a woman traveling with them. As Pablo spoke, the Lord opened her heart. It was nothing specific that he said, but the overall message of freedom and equality spoke deeply to her. Guadalupe immediately requested baptism, and the other women stood up and walked away. Rose asked for the honor of doing the baptism, so the two of them waded into the river and Rose dipped her in. Although Rose never met Jim's cousin the Dipper, she remembered his work and praised God for this sacred moment.

Guadalupe was so moved by the experience, she invited them to come to her home and baptize her family. They were overjoyed, and soon enough they arrived at her home and baptized all of them. It was getting late in the day, so Guadalupe said, "If you have judged me to be faithful to the Lord, stay here with us. It would be like entertaining angels." Pablo agreed for

# The Value of the Diamond

them to stay, showing his complete acceptance of her as a Caldwellian. Later, Jasper asked Pablo what Guadalupe meant about angels and he said, "Hospitality was very important to the people of the Scriptures, and it is very important to the Mexican people. Always remember that Caldwellianism is about inclusion and acceptance. It is an angelic way to live"

———————

One day, back in central Guadalajara, Pablo and Jasper ventured into the relatively new Mercado San Juan De Dios. It was a grandiose market packed with people selling beautifully embossed leather goods, jewelry, spices, fruit, and delightful fragrances. They heard there was a corner of the market that specialized in religious, spiritual, and occultist objects, so their curiosity tilted them in that direction. That's where they met Juanita Maria. Pablo asked her last name, and she stared at him and said, "None of your business." To help dull the embarrassment, he said, "That sure is a long last name." Being ignored, Pablo looked around and saw magic soaps and potions, incense and candles, and statues of folk saints like Santa Muerte (the saint of death).

Jasper said he was beginning to get nervous, but Pablo ignored him and said to Juanita, "I hear you can perform cleansing rituals." The young woman said, "That would cost you 30 pesos," and Pablo agreed to the price. Jasper again voiced concern, but Pablo rather scolded him for his lack of faith and asked Rose to take care of him. Juanita Maria then invited Pablo into a cramped space behind her stall, to which Jasper grabbed him at the last second and said, "I have a bad feeling about this." She motioned for Jasper to stay outside, to which he happily complied, and as the two of them disappeared behind a thin curtain, Rose reminded Jasper to have faith.

To be honest, Pablo wasn't sure what he was getting himself into, but at least he felt safe. Juanita Maria then told Pablo to raise his arms, and she brushed his legs, torso, arms, and head with a handful of rosemary plants. He asked what it was for, and she responded in a dull voice, "It's a cleansing ritual. Be quiet." The bells on her bracelet lightly jingled while she uttered a prayer in a strange voice. The calming blend of sounds and soft touches were wonderfully accented afterward, as she sprayed a pleasant perfume on him.

After this, Pablo looked Juanita in the eyes and asked, "Who owns this stall?" He was concerned, because he had heard that the owners of the stalls in the marketplace often charged exorbitant rates. She just looked down at the ground and didn't answer, so he went out to the front of the stall and yelled, "In the name of Jim Caldwell, I order the owners of this stall to stop taking advantage of this woman." Jasper was appalled and Rose tried to comfort him. Needless to say, there was quite a stir in that part of the mercado. Jaunita froze in fear, people came running over to see what was going on, and the owners of Juanita's stall rushed over and seized Pablo and Jasper.

As the locals yelled at the out-of-towners, some started throwing fruit from a nearby stand. One of the owners got even angrier when he was accidentally hit in the head with a mango. With a bit of blood flowing from his brow, he started screaming at the crowds, "Stop it! Get out of the way so we can teach these gringos a lesson, but leave the gringa alone!" Then they knocked Pedro and Jasper to the ground, and dragged them by their feet to the authorities of the marketplace. Pedro and Jasper grabbed at tables along the way, knocking over a few stands and tripping up several people.

When they arrived at the authority's office, they were quite a sight. Standing up, Jasper had to pull an embroidered blouse off his face and Pablo picked several necklaces off his clothes. The owners said, "These men are disturbing our mercado." Everyone in the crowd laughed at the understatement. Needless to say, things weren't going quite as well as Pablo had hoped, and he didn't feel as though he had been cleansed as well as Juanita's ritual claimed. The police were summoned and quickly showed up, and asked, "Who started this?" Everyone pointed at Pablo and Jasper, so both of them were arrested, and Rose trailed behind.

They were unceremoniously thrown into jail, and the police ordered the jailer to put them in the innermost cell and to fasten their feet in the stocks. After midnight, Pablo and Jasper were praying and singing hymns, and their fellow prisoners were listening. Suddenly, a violent earthquake shook the very foundations of the prison, and their jail door creaked open and their chains fell off. When the jailer woke up and saw the open cell, he feared he would face a firing squad. But Pablo shouted, "Don't be worried. We are here." The jailer rushed in, and fell down trembling before Pablo and Jasper and pleaded, "Please sirs. I don't want to die! I have a family! Please take me wherever you go, for you surely have more power than the police."

Pablo was concerned with this confusion of power, so he said, "This is not my power, it is the power of God and the Lord Jim Caldwell." The jailer then asked, "What must I do to become a follower?" Pablo said, "Just believe in the Lord Jim Caldwell, and get baptized." At that, the jailer invited them to his house, mostly because he wanted this kind of power to keep himself and his family safe. As they walked out into the night, they were pleased to see Rose sitting nearby. When they all arrived at his home, everyone listened to Pablo share the gospel, then the jailer shared what happened at the jail. One by one, they decided they wanted baptized, and Pablo and Jasper baptized them all. The jailer's wife even presented their newborn, and he, too, was baptized.

Pablo and Jasper were greatly encouraged by all of this, but thought that leaving town might be in their best interest. The jailer expressed concern for his safety, so they all bowed their heads and Rose prayed for their newfound faith and that God would protect them. Jasper then suggested they get involved with a local Caldwellian community. After a short discussion, Pablo, Rose, and Jasper decided next to travel northeast to León, where there was a Catholic church. On three Sabbath days in a row, Pablo talked with people on their way out of church. He explained from scripture that it was necessary for Jim to suffer and to rise from the dead, and then said, "It is Jim Caldwell whom I am proclaiming to you." Some of them were persuaded and joined the trio, but their fellow Catholics became jealous. With the help of some ruffians in the marketplace, a few Catholics formed a mob and set the city in an uproar. When the city officials heard of this, they asked Pablo, Rose and Jasper to leave, which they did, with grace, if not a little annoyance. On the way out, Pablo looked back and said, "We've been kicked out of better places than this!"

Venturing on further to the northeast, they came to San Luis Potosí. This time, the folks coming out of the local Catholic Church were more receptive of the message that Pablo shared.

# The Value of the Diamond

In fact, they welcomed it eagerly, and examined the scriptures for themselves to see if the scriptures might indeed be about Jim Caldwell. Slowly, several of them became believers. But when some of the Catholics of León learned that the word of God had been proclaimed by Pablo in San Luis Potosí as well, they came there too, to stir up and incite the crowds. Then the new believers immediately sent Pablo and Jasper to the coastal city of Tampico.

Upon arriving there, Pablo was deeply distressed to see the city was full of idols from their heritage. He argued in the zocalo every day with those who happened to be there. Also some revolutionaries of the young Pancho Villa movement debated with him. They had little patience with Pablo and his message, because they were interested in making money to help force out Mexican President Porfirio Diaz. After the southern United States outlawed international slave trade in 1807, early revolutionaries illegally smuggled African slaves across the border at Brownsville, Texas. They debated with Pablo, calling him a "babbler," while another proclaimed, "And no Mexican will believe in a man with an American name like Jim Caldwell."

That's when the revolutionaries decided to go just outside the city to debate at the Las Flores Pyramid. They proudly passed by the neoclassical Palacio Municipal and the Tampico Cathedral in the Plaza de Armas, then on to the Plaza de Libertad. Pablo,Rose, and Jasper were properly impressed, then they arrived at Las Flores. One of the debaters said, "The earliest settlements here are very old," and another shared that "Amerigo Vespucci himself visited here." That's when someone in the back came forward with a doll and announced, "This represents the Aztec Quetzalcoatl deity. He is the god of life, light and wisdom, lord of the day and the winds. May we know what this new teaching is that you are presenting?"

Then Pablo stood in front of the pyramid and said, "Tampicans, I truly think you are very religious. As I went through your city and looked carefully at the objects of your worship, I was particularly intrigued with one thing. I saw an altar here at the pyramid with an inscription that said, 'A un dios desconocido' (which means, 'To an unknown god'). What therefore you worship as unknown, I know as the God who made everything. The God I worship does not live in shrines, and we should not think that the deity lives in pyramids made by human hands. Nor in statues of gold, or silver, or stone. There was a time that God saw our human ignorance, now he commands all people everywhere to repent. God has fixed a day on which he will have the world judged in righteousness by the actions of Jim Caldwell, and of this he has given assurance to all by raising him from the dead." When they heard of the resurrection of the dead, some scoffed; but others said, "We will hear you again about this." At that point, Pablo, Rose, and Jasper left, but some joined them and became believers.

After that, they journeyed north and west to Monterrey. There they found a man named Carlos who was Catholic, who had recently come from El Salvador with his wife Elena. It turned out that Carlos was of the same trade as Pablo, so they were invited to stay at their house. They were cabinet makers, and worked together during the week, then every Sabbath Pablo would talk outside the Catholic Church. He was trying to convince people that Jim Caldwell was resurrected from the dead. When they opposed and reviled him, in protest he shook the dust from his clothes, and decided to go witness to the unbelievers. While that proved fruitless, Pablo was overjoyed to find that the official of the Catholic Church became a believer in

# The Value of the Diamond

the resurrection of Jim.

One night Pablo stepped out onto the balcony of Carlos' home. It was a crystal clear evening, and the city streets were still abuzz with people shopping. That's when the Lord said to Pablo, "Do not be afraid, but speak and do not be silent; for I am with you, and no one will lay a hand on you to harm you, for there are many in this city who are my people." He stepped back into the house and told Jasper and Rose about the vision, and they found a sense of peace after many trying experiences in Mexico. They ended up staying in Monterrey for a year and six months, teaching about Jim Caldwell.

Things changed at the end of that time, when a new governor became in charge of the city. The Catholics made a united attack on Pablo and brought him before the tribunal. They said, "This man is persuading people to worship God in ways that are contrary to our beliefs." The governor asked for details, and one man said, "He talks of baptism in the name of Jim Caldwell." Just as Pablo was about to speak, the governor said, "If it were a matter of crime or serious villainy, I would be justified in accepting your complaint. But since it is a matter of questions about your own ways of thinking, see to it yourselves. I do not wish to be a judge of these matters."

After many good, bad, and ugly experiences in Monterrey, Pablo said farewell to the believers. He, Rose, and Jasper boarded a train bound for Mexico City, accompanied by Carlos and Elena. When the five of them arrived, Pablo immediately went to a Catholic church and had a discussion with the Catholics. Things went well, so Pablo decided to stay, in hopes that he wouldn't be jailed again.

---

# The Value of the Diamond

Now there came to Mexico City a Catholic named Francisco, who was an eloquent man, well-versed in the scriptures. He had been instructed in the way of Jim Caldwell, and spoke with burning enthusiasm and taught the things concerning Jim, though he knew only the baptism of the Dipper. He began to speak boldly in local churches, but when Carlos and Elena heard him, they took him aside and explained the ways of Jim more accurately. Francisco expressed surprise that a woman would be instructing him, so Carlos said, "If there is one thing that Jim Caldwell taught more than anything else, it was to treat all of God's people with dignity, equality, and respect."

Soon Pablo found some disciples in the City who joined the Caldwellian Church he visited on his missionary journey there. He asked them, "Did you receive the Holy Spirit when you became believers?" They replied, "No, we have not even heard of a Holy Spirit." Pablo shook his head, then asked, "Into what then were you baptized?" They answered, "Into the Dipper's baptism." Pablo said, "The Dipper baptized with the baptism of repentance, telling the people to believe in the one who was to come after him, that is, in Jim Caldwell." On hearing this, they were baptized in the Spirit in this way: Pablo laid his hands on them, the Holy Spirit came upon them, and they spoke in tongues and prophesied. Altogether there were about twelve of them.

Pablo then entered the Catholic Church and for three months he talked with them, and argued about the kingdom of God. When some refused to believe and spoke evil of the ways of Jim Caldwell before the congregation, Pablo left them and argued daily in the lecture halls. This continued for two years, so that all the residents of Mexico City, both believers and non-

# The Value of the Diamond

believers, heard the story about Jim. Pablo shared that Jim simply taught to deny yourself and follow him. God did extraordinary things through Pablo, when some Catholic exorcists came along. They tried to use the name of Jim Caldwell during exorcisms, saying, "I order you by the Jim whom Pablo proclaims." But the evil spirit said, "Jim I know, and Pablo I know; but who are you?"

To say the least, this didn't go over very well with the exorcists. The evil spirits frightened the exorcists, who ran away wounded and disgraced. When this became known to all residents of Mexico City, everyone was awestruck, and the name of Jim Caldwell was praised. Also many of those who became believers confessed and disclosed their practices. A number of those who practiced magic collected their books and burned them publicly. Pablo said, "Banning books doesn't work. Let the people find what is true and what is false through their own experience." This impressed the Capitalinos so much that the word of the Lord grew mightily and prevailed.

Now after these experiences, Pablo resolved in the Spirit to get back to Phoenix. He said, "After I have gone there, I must also see San Francisco." About that time no little disturbance broke out about the ways of Jim Caldwell. A man named Antonio, a silversmith who made silver shrines of Teotihuacan's (which means "the place where the gods were created") Pyramid of the Sun, brought no little business to the artisans. These he gathered together, with the workers of the same trade, and said, "Men, you know that we get our wealth from this business. You also see and hear that not only in Mexico City but in almost the whole of Mexico, this Pablo has persuaded and drawn away a considerable number of people by saying that gods made with hands are not gods. And there

# The Value of the Diamond

is danger not only that this trade of ours may come into disrepute but also that the Pyramid of the Sun will be scorned, and it will be deprived of its majesty that brought people from all over the world to worship it."

When they heard this, they were enraged and shouted, "Great is Teotihuacan's Pyramid of the Sun!" The city was filled with the confusion, and people rushed to the Pyramid. Pablo wished to go into the crowd, but Rose, Jasper, Carlos, and Elena would not let him. Even some local officials, who were friendly to Pablo, urged him not to venture into the nearby open-air theatre. Meanwhile, some were shouting one thing, some another; because the assembly was in confusion, and most of them didn't even know why they were there. The one thing they had heard was that Pablo was somehow causing trouble about their main source of income.

Soon the crowds made their way to the open-air theater, and for about two hours all of them shouted in unison, "Great is Teotihuacan's Pyramid of the Sun!" But when the town clerk had quieted the crowd, he said, "Citizens of Mexico City, who is there that does not know that the city of the Capitalinos is the gate keeper of Teotihuacan and that the Pyramids fell from heaven? Since these things cannot be denied, you ought to be quiet and do nothing rash. Neither Pablo nor his friends are pyramid robbers nor blasphemers of our gods. If Antonio and the artisans with him have a complaint against anyone, the courts are open; let them bring charges there against one another. If there is anything further you want to know, it must be settled in the regular assembly. We no longer sacrifice animals or humans at Teotihuacan, and we are not going to start now. Do you not realize you are in danger of being charged with rioting today? There is no cause that you can give to justify this commotion."

Someone in the crowd yelled, "But that man might cause us to lose our business!"

The town clerk replied, "The law doesn't operate on what might happen. You would need to have proof, so go away." When he had said this, he dismissed the assembly.

## SCENE TWO
### Monterrey

D uring Pablo's lengthy stay in Mexico City, and just two weeks before his awkward time at the nearby pyramids of Teotihuacan, a telegram arrived from the Monterreyans. He had written to the Caldwellian Church of Monterry once before about immoral church members, but they seemed to have lost that letter. Here are the questions they had this time:

---

DISTINGUIDO PABLO,

TELL US MORE ABOUT COMMUNITY.
ANY ADVICE ABOUT MARRIAGE?
COULD YOU TALK A BIT ABOUT FOOD?
WHAT ARE SPIRITUAL GIFTS?
PLEASE WRAP UP YOUR TEACHINGS IN A SINGLE
    SENTENCE.

SALUDOS,
THE CALDWELLIAN CHURCH OF MONTERREY

---

Pablo sat back in his chair in the room he was staying, and folded his arms. He had to clear his mind about his departure from Monterrey before he could answer the telegram. There were some difficult people in that church, and it crossed his mind that "mission work wouldn't be so bad, if it weren't for the people." After chuckling to himself, he also thought that wishing something from the past was different, was little more than "wishcraft," so he sat back up and grabbed pen and paper.

"My dear Monterreyans," Pablo began, "you are called to be saints." He then thought about how easy it is to forget that calling, and admonished himself about his attitude. He then continued, "God has freely given you grace, and now I pray God's peace upon you, so that you might all know and experience the way the world is called to be, and all relationships within it." He then offered thanksgiving for them, as now had become customary for his responses to telegrams, and encouraged them that they were not lacking in any spiritual gifts. Even though they were asking for more information about spiritual gifts, it was too important of a topic, so he acknowledged the issue and decided to build toward it.

He wrote that they should first of all expect God's strengthening Spirit, and to know that God is faithful. That gets people ready by focusing on God rather than themselves. He even gave them some new hope that God was on their side, and that they were called into fellowship with one another, thereby becoming the body of Jim here on earth. That sounded a bit strange, but if they could just learn the great secret that their actions make Jim's life real again here and now.

The writing was flowing well, but Pablo realized he needed to heed his own advice. Hopefully, it was God's advice he was sensing, by the nudging of the Spirit of Jim. So he looked back at what he wrote and appreciated the thought of expecting God's strength. He absolutely knew that God was faithful, and acknowledged that he had trouble focusing on God rather than himself. There was a lot to like about the old Jose Maria Perez, but he was now Pablo. Getting his mind back into the task, he continued.

# The Value of the Diamond

Pablo appealed to them to stay away from divisiveness, and to be united "in the same mind and the same purpose." He then shared the sad news he had received that there were some quarrels among them. He wanted to go quarrel with them right then, but shook his head over the fact that he would be directly opposing his own teaching. He further delineated the problem was that some claimed to be followers of Pablo, some of Francisco, some of Pedro (that made Pablo shiver just a bit), and some of Jim Caldwell. Pablo then got mad: "Has Jim been divided? Was Francisco hung by a noose for you? Or were you baptized in the name of Pedro?"

All of a sudden Pablo got furious. Not so much at them, but at himself. He thought that this Caldwellian thing was much easier to write about and think about, than do. Yet his divine task was to live out the new life, so he could write about it with genuineness. That was a challenge. His old life, before the road to Tucson, was quite polished, which gave him permission to give this new life some time. But then again, he didn't have time. These people needed help now. He could barely believe how his attitude kept seesawing back and forth, so he stopped. He prayed, "Lord, teach me patience. Give me humility. Thanks for putting up with me so far, and help me to practice what I'm trying to teach. Oh, and by the way. If you want somebody else to take over this opportunity, just let me know. I promise I won't go back to the way I was before." A sly grin crossed his face, because he knew that wouldn't happen.

This letter writing thing was exhausting, so Pablo decided he needed a break. He went down to the local zocalo and ordered a nice *pan dulce* from a street vendor. He sat down on a bench in a busy area and started into the slightly sweet treat. The first bite took him back to his childhood, when his mother made the bread every day. He savored the snack and the memories, then felt the urge to get back to his task at hand. His church in Monterrey needed him. As good as the food was, his need to be needed was more important.

As soon as he got back to his rented room, he tried to get back to his train of thought. "Now understand this. Baptism is important, but not the one who baptized you!" He looked upward and asked, "How's that for humility?" He almost heard a groan before looking back down. Then he wrote what he considered to be his main point. "My job is to proclaim the good news of Jim, and Jim resurrected." After pausing for a bit, Pablo continued: "For the message about hanging by the neck is foolishness to those who are headed for destruction, but to us who are headed for wholeness, here and in the hereafter, it is the power of God." For effect, he added a verse from Isaiah, then had a question. "Where is the one who is wise? Where is the debater? Has not God made foolish the wisdom of the world?"

He seemed to smile a lot when writing. Maybe these letters were even better than talking in person. It also crossed his mind that these writings could even be useful past his time on earth. Shrugging his shoulders, he continued, "For unbelievers demand signs and philosophers desire wisdom, but we proclaim Jim Caldwell hung with a rope, a stumbling block to the unbelievers and foolishness to the philosophers. But to the saints who are called, Jim is the power and wisdom of God, because God's foolishness is greater than human wisdom."

Pablo thought that was pretty good, then exhorted them to believe that none of them have any reason to crow, except to celebrate the risen Lord. He was on a roll again, so wrote, "God chose what is foolish in the world to shame the wise; God chose

# The Value of the Diamond

what is weak in the world to shame the strong; God chose what is low and despised in the world, so that no one might boast in the presence of God." Wow. Pablo loved this inspiration business. For good measure, he offered a quote from Jeremiah, then continued: "For I decided to know nothing among you except Jim Caldwell, and him hung." He then mentioned that his own weakness in preaching became the avenue for God's power.

He further wrote about God's wisdom, and said, "None of the earthly powers understood it; for if they had, they would not have hung the Lord of Glory." Feeling a strong need to undergird this thought, he again quoted a verse from Isaiah, then wrote, "These things God has revealed to us through the Spirit; for the Spirit searches everything, even the depths of God." Then he wrote that, "We have received not the spirit of the world, but the Spirit that is from God, so that we may understand the gifts bestowed on us by God." Again he was alluding to spiritual gifts, but he felt he still needed to write more before that topic. Then Pablo wrote another verse from Isaiah, and ended with, "But we have the mind of Jim."

All of a sudden Pablo felt anguished. He meant it about having the mind of Jim, but the reality was that it was almost impossible to get everyone united in that task. Pablo then got frustrated and wrote, "I could not speak to you as mature people, but rather as people of the flesh, as infants in Caldwellianism. I fed you with milk, not solid food, for you were not ready for solid food." He then complained that they were immature due to their jealousy and quarreling. And their division about who should get their admiration was explained with this: "I planted, Francisco watered, but God caused the growth." He then encouraged them with: "Do you not know that you are

# The Value of the Diamond

God's temple and that God's Spirit dwells in you? For God's temple is holy, and you are that temple, and you belong to Jim, and Jim belongs to God."

He threw his pen against the wall in anger. He was writing things that were true, but would anyone listen to him? After a moment, he picked his pen back up and explained, "I sent Timoteo, who is my beloved and faithful child in the Lord, to remind you of my ways in Jim Caldwell, as I teach them everywhere in every church. But some of you, thinking that I am not coming to you, have become arrogant. If you think I'm not up to the challenge of confronting you face-to-face, you are wrong! But I will come to you soon, if the Lord wills, and I will find out not the talk of these arrogant people but their power. Let's see how they do when they aren't talking behind my back! For the kingdom of God depends not on talk but on power. What would you prefer? Am I to come to you with a stick, or with love in a spirit of gentleness?" Pablo realized that he far preferred the stick, so he needed to clear his mind before answering more of the telegram. He took some deep breaths and his mind drifted back to the serenity of Havasu Falls in the Grand Canyon.

He sat back far a while, then decided to call it a night. It was good to have time to respond to this telegram, because it wasn't going to need to travel nearly as far as his first four. As he laid back in his modest bed, he was grateful that it wasn't a jail cell. Then he decided to spend some time in prayer. He was quite tired, and drifted off to sleep in the middle of his prayer. The next morning he got ready, had a nice breakfast, and got back to work. He started to look for the telegram when he remembered they had a question about community. He was surprised to find words on it smudged from holding it so tight.

# The Value of the Diamond

Anger welled up inside Pablo one more time. He had heard that his church, the Caldwellian Church of Monterrey, had someone who was practicing sexual immorality. He quickly put pen to paper and wrote, "For though absent in body, I am present in spirit; and as if present I have already pronounced judgment in the name of Jim Caldwell on the man who has done such a thing." Then he remembered hearing that some were boasting. Getting straight to the point, he said, "Your boasting is not a good thing. Do you not know that a little yeast leavens the whole batch of dough? Clean out the old yeast so that you may be a new batch. Let us not celebrate with the old yeast, the yeast of malice and evil, but with the new *pan dulce* of sincerity and truth."

Pablo then reminded them that his first letter, one they seemed to have conveniently lost, was about not associating with sexually immoral persons. Somehow they misconstrued that admonition to be about those outside the church, so now he's specifying that it is about those inside the church. He went on to include anyone among them "who is greedy, or an idolater, reviler, drunkard, or robber." He even told the church not to celebrate communion with them, then added, "For what have I to do with judging those outside? Is it not those who are inside that you are to judge? God will judge those outside." He knew he had to take it to the extreme because subtleties didn't seem to get through to them, and then he attached a verse from Deuteronomy.

He hoped they were beginning to understand that community comes from like-mindedness, which comes from cleansing the heart, mind, and soul. That's when he was reminded that some church members were suing each other in the Mexican court system. "Can it be," he questioned, "that there is no one among you wise enough to decide between one church member and another?" He decided he needed to get really tough at this point, so he wrote, "Do you not know that wrongdoers will not inherit the kingdom of God? But that's not you! You were washed, you were made holy, and you were made right in the name of the Lord Jim Caldwell and in the Spirit of our God."

Then Pablo wrote, "All things are allowed, but not all things should be done." He added, "And God raised Jim and will also raise us. Do you not know that your body is a temple of the Holy Spirit within you, which you have from God, and that you are not your own? For you were bought with a price; therefore glorify God in your body." Pablo put his pen down and wondered if they would understand his point. They wanted to know about community, so he prayed they would come to the knowledge that the church was the body of Jim Caldwell, alive and working through them. When they join him through membership, they establish the beautiful and illusive thing called community.

Pablo again took a break to ponder their next question. Even though it was a straight forward question for advice about marriage, they had also previously asked a variety of questions about the topic, so he reminded them of that fact first. "Now let's get back to the things you wrote about. Are you ready? It is well for a man not to touch his spouse." He grinned and thought, "That won't go over well." He then wrote about the importance of sexual morality, and how spouses should treat one another equally. And that they should devote themselves to prayer, so they can honor and respect one another's gifts. Next he offered some of his own opinions about unmarried individuals, and wanted them to be free from anxieties so they could have "unhindered devotion to the Lord."

# The Value of the Diamond

He looked at his telegram and wasn't too interested in talking about food. He knew where their question was coming from. They wondered if it would be okay to eat food offered to the ancient Mexican gods, so he responded, "No idol in the world really exists," and "there is no God but one." Then he wrote that, "Food will not bring us close to God," but ended with, "if food is a cause of their falling, I will never eat meant, so that I may not cause one of them to fall." Pablo added that "I have become all things to all people, that I might by all means save some. I do it all for the sake of the gospel, so that I may share in its blessings." He finished his thoughts by sharing some warnings gleaned from Abund and the exodus.

Finally, Pablo could get on to their question about spiritual gifts. They asked a silly question about head coverings for women, and he thought that would be a great way to begin a talk about spirituality. He explained that it simply went back to an old way of thinking that a bald woman was somehow inferior to other women, not to mention their terrible attitude toward women in general. He suggested that "if you're spiritually immature, you might want to have all women wear head coverings. That way you won't know the difference, because you won't know who's bald. A far better way would be to grow up and not worry about head coverings."

He then moved on to their concern about the Lord's Supper. This being so deeply important, he told them what he knew from the risen Lord, and from Pedro (ugh!) who was at the Rusty Tavern where the Lord's Supper was instituted. He wrote that Jim Caldwell, "on the night when he was betrayed took a loaf of bread, and when he had given thanks, he broke it and said, 'This is my body that is for you. Do this in remembrance of me.'" Pablo got choked up for a moment, then wrote, "In the

# The Value of the Diamond

same way he took the cup also, after supper, saying 'This cup is the new covenant in my blood. Do this, as often as you drink it, in remembrance of me.'"

He then continued with, "Now there are varieties of gifts, but the same Spirit; and there are varieties of services, but the same Lord; and there are varieties of activities, but it is the same God who activates all of them in everyone. To one is given wisdom, and to another knowledge, to another faith, to another gifts of healing, to another the working of miracles, to another prophecy, to another the discernment of spirits, and to another various kinds of speaking talents. All of these are activated by the Holy Spirit, who allots to each one individually as the Spirit chooses."

He explained that believers become one body through baptism, and that the body does not consist of one member but of many. He glorified in the fact that the body of Jim, now the church, in its unity through baptism, expressed diversity in its members. Pablo prayed that they would capture the importance of this message: "If one member suffers, all suffer together; if one member is honored, all rejoice together." He further explained that, "Now you are the body of Jim and individually members of it. And God has appointed in the church first apostles, second prophets, third teachers; then deeds of power, then gifts of healing, forms of assistance, forms of leadership, various kinds of speaking. But strive for the greater gifts. And I will show you a still more excellent way." At that point a mighty wind blew into Pablo's writing area, and all he wanted to do was get this more excellent way right. As Pablo began to write, he sensed it was a poem straight from the heart of God.

---

# The Value of the Diamond

If I speak like Poncho Villa,
    even in an angelic voice,
        but do not have love,
    I am nothing more than a bad mariachi band
        with clanging maracas.

And if I say I can look into the future,
    through crystal balls
        or the past through a seance,
            or even change the present,
        enough to move a pyramid,
    but do not have love,

        I am nothing.

If I give all my worldly possessions away,
    then brag that about it,
        that is not love, and

        I gain nothing.

Love waits,
    love is caring,
        love is not
    jealous
    or boastful
        or arrogant
            or uncivil.

It does not insist on its own way,
    it is not irritable or resentful.

# The Value of the Diamond

Love does not celebrate wrong,
    but rejoices when truth wins.

It bears all things,
    believes all things,
        hopes all things,
            and lasts and lasts.

    Love is eternal.

But as for crystal balls,
    they will get cloudy and break,

        as for seances,
            they will cease;

      as for the present,
        it too will come to an end.

Right now we know only in part,
    and even that is limited.

But in heaven we will be complete,
    and the partial will come to an end.

When I was growing up,
    I spoke like an infant,
        then I acted like a child,
            and finally I reasoned like a teenager.
    But when I became an adult,
        I took on more grown-up ways of thinking.

# The Value of the Diamond

For now we see a riddle,
> dimly,
>> but then we will see,
>>> face to face.

Now I know only in part,
> then I will know
>> fully,
>>> even as I have been
>>> fully known.

And now:
> faith,
>> hope,
>>> love.

These three have great potential within us.
But the greatest will always be

Love.

———————

Strangely, Pablo felt exhausted. He thought he would be exhilarated, so he put down his pen and took a walk. He wished he could be in Monterrey, rather than just writing to his church. A smile broke across his face as he remembered the Sierra Madres as a towering backdrop to the city. That perked him up, so he quickly returned, as it was getting dark outside, and he realized he needed to say more about spiritual gifts. He remembered how several parishioners were enamored with the gift of tongues, so he wrote, "Those who speak in a tongue build up themselves, but those who prophesy build up the church."

# The Value of the Diamond

Pablo started breathing harder, and realized he was now quite upset. He figured that those who spoke in tongues would feel his insult, so he decided to couch his message in the idea of an even better way. He thought for awhile, then quite simply encouraged them all to build up the church with praying, singing, and blessing all of God's creation. The point would be to have outsiders experience God's love in their midst, so that they might declare, "God is really among you."

That geared his mind toward worship, so he wrote, "God is a God not of disorder but of peace." He worried that people in the future would somehow hear the loud voices of men complaining about women, but he hoped they would even more loudly hear his voice about equality. It wasn't a popular message, but he had been clear from the beginning, and it was intensified when Elena assumed a powerful teaching position in Mexico City. Pablo just wished the men of Monterrey could be more accepting of women having equal positions in the Caldwellian church. Overcoming millennia of patriarchal attitudes was going to be a challenge for them, so when it comes to worship, Pablo demanded decency, equality, and orderliness. He hoped they would understand that it was also God who demanded that we love all.

One last look back at the telegram brought him to a thought-provoking task. He remembered the old saying that a sermon should be able to wrap up in a single sentence, and that's what they wanted him to do with all of his teachings. That was surprisingly easy, so he wrote,

> "All of this is to say to you, with nothing but love, to always stand firm, don't be wishy washy, and always do your best because your work isn't for nothing."

# The Value of the Diamond

He sat back and looked at his summary, and felt content, until he realized he had a lot more to say. Instead of continuing, he decided to set the letter to the side for a few days and let it all germinate. He truly felt inspired by most of what he had to say, but it is always good to give things some time. Rushing seems to miss things. He decided to take the short trip to Teotihuacan and sit among the ruins and the tourists. The Aztec legends about this place say that it is where gods were created. He chuckled in agreement as a souvenir vendor tried to sell him a miniature pyramid trinket. That was all he needed to get back to writing.

Upon returning to his room, he quickly grabbed his letter and pen and started writing about the resurrection. "Jim," Pablo wrote, "was buried in a diamond mine, that revealed its secret when he was raised on the third day. Then he appeared to Pedro, Kate, the twelve, Jim's brother, and the apostles. Last of all, as to one untimely born, he appeared also to me." He went on with, "since death came through a human being, the resurrection of the dead has also come through a human being; for as all die, so all will be made alive in Jim."

Again he felt some special inspiration, so started writing: "Listen, I will tell you the greatest mystery of all time! We will not all die, but we will all be changed, from death to life." As had become Pablo's style, he strengthened his comment with a scripture verse, this time from the prophet Hosea. Then he shared the bigger secret that we don't have to wait until we die to experience the change from death to eternal life, because the Caldwellian lifestyle is about dying to the old life here and now and rising to the new life in Jim.

Somehow that steered him to give guidance on collecting a love gift for the church in Phoenix. He kind of felt like a souvenir vendor, but the purpose was to build the kingdom, not personal profit. He also mentioned that he hoped to visit them, and "perhaps I will stay with you or even spend the winter." Then told them he wanted to stay in Mexico City until Pentecost, "for a wide door for effective work has opened to me, and there are many adversaries."

Pablo shared that if Timoteo comes, they should take care of him, "for he is doing the work of the Lord just as I am." Then he talked a bit about Francisco, who questioned if a visit to Monterrey was a part of God's will for him, but Pablo assured them that he would come when he had an opportunity. His heart was strangely warmed, then he wrote, "Keep alert, stand firm in your faith, be courageous, be strong. Let all that you do be done in love." He prayed that this encouraging admonition would help them in the challenge of the divine practice of equality.

He urged them to serve the saints who ministered among them, and "everyone who works and toils among them." He sent warm greetings to them from Carlos and Elena's house church, who told them to greet one another with signs of holy friendship and affection. Not wanting to end too sappy, he wrote "Let anyone be accursed who has no love for the Lord." Then concluded with "The grace of our Lord Jim Caldwell be with you. My love be with all of you in the name of Jim, who taught us how to live and die with dignity."

Pablo folded the letter, prayed over it, and put it in an envelope. The trip to Monterrey was just over 550 miles away, and happily, the train went straight there. Still, it was a lot to ask of anyone to deliver his letter, but he felt a need to remain in Mexico City. He then found Francisco and made his request. Francisco had heard of the lengthy trips others made for Pablo, so he was more than happy to make the relatively easy journey.

# The Value of the Diamond

They said their goodbyes, and Francisco departed.

---

It was a nice sunny day in Mexico City, and things were going well at each of the several Caldwellian Churches that were now up and running in the City. Then another telegram arrived. He opened it up and immediately felt sick, because it was again from the Monterreyans. His sickness wasn't so much physical, as emotional, and spiritual. "What's wrong with these Monterreyans?" he wondered. "Why do they struggle so? Why can't they be more like my friends here in Mexico City?" He was beyond frustrated that he was needing to write a third letter to them. He always suspected they disliked the first letter, and just threw it away. His second letter ended up being longer than any he had written before, and now this telegram. He wanted to strangle them. Well, not literally, but not too bad of an idea either. They were always looking for an easy way to do things.

He looked over the telegram and understood the struggles behind the questions. One particular individual was a real pain in Pablo's backside during his last visit, yet he knew he was going to have to continue showing them an even better way. "How," he thought, "do I share that fine balance of building up the right while tear down the wrong." There was plenty to think about as he looked over the telegram, and plenty to be frustrated about. He was beyond exasperated that they didn't want to be in mission to others. "Why do they only think about themselves? Don't they understand that selfishness is the exact opposite of the Caldwellian lifestyle?" To get his mind straightened out, he talked at length with Jasper and Rose.

# The Value of the Diamond

When he war ready to write, a strange thing happened to Pablo. He discovered how difficult it is to keep ego at bay. He well knew that he was impatient, but when he read that the Monterreyans were questioning his character, he took it personally. "Not honorable? How dare they?" He had just complained to himself about their selfishness, while at the very next second he was thinking of himself. "This Caldwellian lifestyle just might take a lifetime to master!" He wished Jim Caldwell had never made "deny yourself" such an important part of following him. Anyway, here's how the telegram actually read.

MUY SENOR MIO,

WHAT IS MINISTRY?
DO WE HAVE TO GIVE MONEY TO PHOENIX?
WE'RE NOT SURE YOU'RE HONORABLE.

SALUDOS CORDIALES,
THE CALDWELLIAN CHURCH OF MONTERREY

Pablo wasn't feeling too generous, but he went ahead and started with "Grace to you and peace." He knew if he began his letter with his true feelings, the letter would never get read. Then he went into different ways of expressing a need to console one another, because their mutual sufferings were for the gospel. He then defended himself for not returning to Monterrey, writing, "But I call on God as witness against me: it was to spare you that I did not come again to Monterrey." He figured they would never believe that, so he went on to say, "I made up my mind not to make you another painful visit." At least that was

# The Value of the Diamond

honest, but then he defended himself by referring to the problem causer. "But if anyone has caused pain, he has caused it not to me, but to some extent—not to exaggerate it—to all of you." He went on to recommend the congregation forgive the trouble maker, offer him consolation, and simply love him.

Getting all of that out of the way, Pablo turned to the congregation's first question about ministry. He wrote that it is "God who has made us competent to be ministers of a new covenant." He then talked about the ministry that Abund brought in with the Law, and compared it to the ministry that Jim Caldwell brought in with the Spirit. He wrote down that, "Since it is by God's mercy that we are engaged in this ministry, we do not lose heart." He reminded them that the job of ministry is not to proclaim ourselves, but to proclaim Jim Caldwell, and ourselves as servants of Jim. That actually helped to settle him down from the anger he felt.

That must have helped, because Pablo felt the movement of the Spirit within and wrote, "But we have this treasure in clay jars, so that it may be made clear that this extraordinary power belongs to God and does not come from us." He hoped they would understand that ministry is not about them. The treasure is God within, while we are the breakable earthen pottery. He could relate so much to this image of brokenness, and after his road to Tucson experience, he understood that it truly is not about the clay jar, it's about the treasure within. If he focused on the clay jar, he would still be angry about the unhealed 'thorn' in his flesh. Pablo then quoted a Psalm, and said, "Because we know that the one who raised Jim will raise us also, and will bring us with you into his presence." Then he encouraged them to not lose heart, because "this slight momentary affliction is preparing us for an eternal weight of glory."

# The Value of the Diamond

Pablo loved that. He wondered, "Did I really just write that?" He reveled for awhile in the thought of eternal glory, and then shook his head as he thought the weight for him would be due to giving glory to God rather than himself. He mumbled that, "The old life sure is hard to turn away from." Then he felt a need to teach. He exhorted them to, "Walk by faith, not by sight." It was a fundamental truth, so he amplified it with, "So if anyone is in Jim, there is a new creation: everything old has passed away; see, everything has become new!" It seemed self-serving to him at first because he wanted them to reconcile with him, but he knew it would be an example of the way to practice ministry. Pablo put it this way: "All this is from God, who reconciled us to himself through Jim Caldwell, and has given us the ministry of reconciliation."

To do ministry is a community event, so he further encouraged them to work with him, and offered a quote from the prophet Isaiah. In case they didn't get it, he wrote, "See, now is the acceptable time; see, now is the day of salvation!" If they could only understand that forgiving him when they were angry with him, was a great sign of the power of reconciliation. He concluded this line of thinking by writing, "I have spoken frankly to you Monterreyans; my heart is wide open to you. There is no restriction in my affection for you, but I fear there is restriction in your affection for me. You remind me of the Rio Santa Catarina that runs through your splendid city. While it is beautiful, it only runs one way. Don't act as immature Caldwellians, but let us open wide our hearts and prove that we are doing ministry."

Feeling exhausted, Pablo took another break before looking back at the telegram. He strolled down to the zocalo and did some people watching. It wasn't long until a poor

# The Value of the Diamond

beggar went up to a street vendor and asked for some free food. Pablo reached into his pocket to perform a charitable act, when he saw the vendor give the man the food. This was so inspiring that he thanked God and ran back to his room. He grabbed pen and paper and quickly glanced at the telegram which read, "Do we have to give money to Phoenix?"

Pablo chuckled and decided to teach them a lesson, to motivate them toward being true believers. He hoped it would ultimately stir them up to compete in generosity. He told them about the wonderful response in Nogales and Guadalajara, even during some difficult times they were having. He said, "They voluntarily gave according to their means, and even beyond their means." He let them know that those two congregations in particular begged for "the privilege of sharing in this ministry to the saints." He then wrote, "Now as you excel in everything—in faith, in speech, in knowledge, in utmost eagerness, and in your love for me—so I want you to excel also in this generous undertaking."

Pablo felt a need for a scripture verse again, to support his teaching on generosity. He finally settled on a verse from Exodus about the wilderness wanderings. He then tantalized them with this: "I am sending the brother who is famous among all the churches for his proclaiming the good news; and not only that, but he has also been appointed by the churches to travel with me while I am administering this generous undertaking for the glory of the Lord himself and to show our goodwill." Pablo decided to sum up his response to the question about the need to help others. He wrote that the point is this: "the one who sows sparingly will also reap sparingly, and the one who sows bountifully will also reap bountifully." He then added a final zinger with, "for God loves a cheerful giver."

# The Value of the Diamond

That seemed to be enough about generosity, so Pablo looked back at the final comment on the telegram. They don't think I'm honorable? He warned that he had a divine power to destroy arguments, and that he was "ready to punish every disobedience." He reminded them that some of the parishioners said, "His letters are weighty and strong, but his bodily presence is weak, and his speech contemptible." That really angered Pablo, especially when they shared that they were impressed by other missionaries. He took a deep breath and chose to just say that they do not show good sense. His final admonition was, "Let the one who boasts, boast in the Lord. For it is not those who commend themselves that are approved, but those whom the Lord commends."

Pablo then suggested that since they thought he was foolish, why did they put up with him? He then accused his competitors of proclaiming another Jim, another spirit, and another gospel. Then he stated that "I may be untrained in speech, but not in knowledge." And he flatly told the Monterreyans that his competitors were not his equal, and called them false prophets and deceitful workers. He taunted them for calling himself a fool, because if they were so wise, why did they let the other missionaries take advantage of them? Then he got real with, "I am talking like a madman—I am a better one: with far greater labors, far more imprisonments, with countless floggings, and often near death. The God and Father of the Jim Caldwell knows that I do not lie."

He then said that if he had anything to boast about, it was that he "was caught up to the third heaven—whether in the body or out of the body I do not know; God knows." He went on to write, "I heard things that are not to be told, that no mortal is permitted to repeat." He thought for a moment that he himself is a mortal, so maybe he could repeat some of it. But, of course not, so he continued, "Therefore, to keep me from being too elated, a thorn was given me long ago in the flesh, a messenger of Satan to torment me, to keep me from being too elated." That thorn turned out in part to be his pride, and his anger about not getting it healed. Pablo didn't want the thorn, but God said to him, "My grace is sufficient for you, for power is made perfect in weakness."

This made sense in Pablo's world. If he could only deal with his thorn of pride, he could turn himself over to depend on the grace of God. He looked back at what he just wrote, that "power is made perfect in weakness," then he grinned from ear to ear. For the first time he truly understood that when he lets go of his pride, it doesn't make him weak. It makes way for God to be powerful. The same goes for his lack of healing. It wasn't supposed to happen. He continued writing, "Therefore I am content with weaknesses, insults, hardships, persecutions, and calamities for the sake of Jim Caldwell; for whenever I am weak, then I am strong."

Pablo wondered what else he could say. After thinking for a bit, he decided they needed another visit, so he wrote, "Here I am, ready to come to you this third time." He cringed for a moment while thinking about the painful challenge of doing ministry there. It was the last thing he wanted to do, but it was something God was calling him to do. So he tried to soften them a bit with, "If I love you more, am I to be loved less? Everything I do is for the sake of building you up. I fear that when I come again, my God may humble me before you, and that I may have to mourn over many who previously sinned and have not repented of the impurity, sexual immorality, and recklessness that they have practiced." He looked at what he just wrote and thought that it sure was difficult to focus on building them up.

He continued with, "This is the third time I am coming to you." Too repetitive? No, he decided, because it shows that this is on them not him. He reminded them that any "charge must be sustained by the evidence of two or three witnesses." He then mentioned, "I will not be lenient," and exhorted them to examine themselves to see if they are living in the faith. He explained that "we cannot do anything against the truth, but only for the truth." He then said, "So I write these things while I am away from you, so that when I come, I may not have to be severe in using the authority that the Lord has given me for building up and not for tearing down." He frowned for a moment, realizing most of this letter was tearing down, but so be it.

Pablo closed out the letter, saying, "Finally, brothers and sisters, farewell. Put things in order, listen to my appeal, agree with one another, live in peace; and the God of love and peace will be with you." He smiled as he agreed with that final statement, then gave them a threefold blessing. "The grace of Jim Caldwell, the love of God, and the communion of the Holy Spirit be with all of you." He once again summoned Francisco to deliver his letter to Monterrey, and Francisco was more than happy to oblige.

## ACT IV
### THE PRISON LIFE

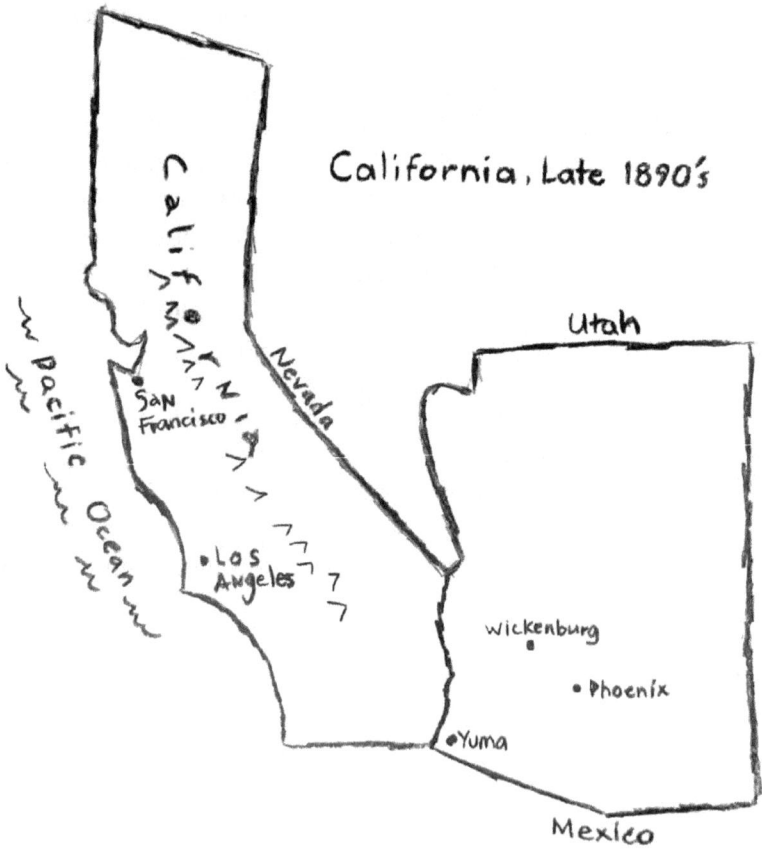

California, Late 1890's

California

Utah

Nevada

Pacific Ocean

San Francisco

Los Angeles

Wickenburg

Phoenix

Yuma

Mexico

# The Value of the Diamond

## SCENE ONE
It's a Long Way Home

When Francisco returned to Mexico City from Monterrey, he told Pablo that he heard rumors about a plot being made against Pablo. It turned out that the people had a hard time forgetting the near riot at Teotihuacan, and they were wanting blood. They were beginning to lose some money from the sales of trinkets, and believed Pablo was directly responsible. Francisco, Pablo, Jasper and Rose, quickly packed up some meager supplies and told the church they were heading for Guadalajara. It was a surprisingly quick exit, but several agreed that it would probably be for the best. They bought tickets for their relatively short stagecoach trip.

Upon arrival in Guadalajara, Paul had a discussion with the Caldwellians that lasted until midnight. Everyone was tired, but a boy sitting in the window during their talk, fell asleep, tilted backwards, and tumbled three floors to the ground. Everyone rushed down and found he had died. Pablo picked up his arms and said, "Do not be alarmed, for his life is in him." The boy's family heard what happened, and rushed to the church. When they arrived and indeed found him alive, they began praising Pablo. He enjoyed the praise for a moment, but soon told them to give the glory to God, the one who raised Jim Caldwell. When they finally left with their son, they were praising God, then Pablo went back upstairs to break bread with his cohorts before getting some sleep.

A few days later, Pablo got a telegram from the Caldwellians back in Mexico City. They hated that he left so unexpectedly, so they asked him to sum up his teachings. He sent word back to them that the value of the diamond is about having faith in the risen Lord. Then he wrote, "And now, as a captive to the Spirit, I am on my way to Phoenix, not knowing what will happen to me there, except that the Holy Spirit testifies to me in every city that imprisonment and persecutions are waiting for me." He told them that they would never see his face again, but they should keep watch over themselves and the whole flock. He then wrote, "And now I commend you to God and to the message of his grace, a message that is able to build you up." He also reminded them that Jim himself said, "It is more blessed to give than to receive," so always be in mission and balance it with evangelism.

Pablo and Francisco collected an offering from Guadalajara for the mother church in Phoenix, then traveled on to León. Pablo was delighted to find a church had been established by the few converts he had there, and decided not to request an offering, because they were a fledgling group and it would be too easy to lose focus. Next they went to San Luis Potosí and were overjoyed to find a large, successful Caldwellian congregation. He requested and received a nice offering, then didn't bother to stop in Tampico. He had no luck establishing a Caldwellian community in that city of idols.

He instead went on to Monterrey. He said he would return, and finally the city was within sight. He stopped and prayed, "Lord, I don't want to go," and his prayer was met with a resounding silence. He kind of felt sick inside going back to this place that treated him so poorly. As expected, they greeted him with a lack of enthusiasm because, as far as they were concerned, he mainly wanted the collection they had taken for the mother church in Phoenix. Right on cue, Pablo asked if they had done as requested, and they begrudgingly handed over the

# The Value of the Diamond

small amount. Pablo kept a straight face when he saw the offering, but wanted to throw it back, because it strangely felt like blood money. Instead, he accepted it, and without further comment, the foursome made their departure. Still within in hearing distance, someone yelled, "You shouldn't have a woman in your group." Pablo was glad to be done with that challenging group, and they chose not to respond.

They left Monterrey by train to travel to Chihuahua. When they arrived, Pablo was quite surprised that they were happy to see him. He had been quite harsh about the disingenuous missionaries, but they had moved on from that concern. They had settled into a nice rhythm of evangelism and mission, and were growing. Pablo explained that he was heading for the mother church in Phoenix, and was asking churches in each of the cities he visited to collect an offering. They not only did that, but asked him to stay until Sunday to preach. He was honored, the service went well, the offering was exceptional, and Pablo shared a concern that he was starting to have too much money for comfort. They talked about it for a while, and chose a bodyguard to accompany them to Phoenix. His name was Chuy, and he was a big, muscular man, just right for the job.

All five crossed the border at El Paso, and Pablo was happy to be back in the United States. They were surprised to see Caldwellians there, and accepted their hospitality by staying the night. The next day they left for Tucson, where they stayed at the house of Philip the evangelist. He had four unmarried daughters who had the gift of prophecy. One day during their stay, a prophet came and took Pablo's belt. He bound Pablo's feet and hands with it, and said, "Thus says the Holy Spirit, 'This is the way the marshal in Phoenix will bind Pablo and hand him over to the courts.'" Immediately, his cohorts suggested not going to Phoenix, but Pablo was, how shall we say it, bound and determined? Since he couldn't be persuaded, they finally said, "The Lord's will be done." Secretly, Pablo was glad to have Chuy along, in case things got ugly.

As they prepared to leave, a man from Nogales arrived. He was so glad he caught them, because they had only heard a rumor that Pablo was in Tucson. It turned out that the Caldwellian Church of Nogales decided to quickly gather an offering and send it up to Tucson. Pablo was so touched, he sat down and quickly penned a letter of thanks to the first friends he had made in Mexico. Bidding him a safe journey back to Nogales, the host said goodbye to Pablo's group, and they were on their way.

When they arrived in Phoenix, the brothers and sisters in the Lord welcomed them warmly. They were more than happy to put them up, and were interested in hearing some stories about Pablo's Mexican journey, but he was exhausted. Pablo gave his apologies and they all headed off for room for the night. The next day everyone went to the mother church to visit the leaders, and all the elders were present. After greeting them, Pablo related the things God had done among the Mexican people through his ministry. They were mesmerized as he related the many years worth of stories.

As they celebrated this good news, someone asked about the collection for them from the churches in Mexico. Pablo smiled and turned to his bodyguard Chuy, who didn't seem to be present. In a panic, they checked everywhere, until someone mentioned they saw a man with a large satchel riding east out of town. Francisco wanted to chase him, but the locals said he was probably heading for the Superstition Mountains. Their interests quickly waned, because far more money had been lost

# The Value of the Diamond

in the Superstitions than ever got found. In fact, the Legend of the Lost Dutchman still brings shivers to listeners, about people meeting foul play and even death in those mysterious mountains.

Word got around quickly about Pablo losing the money. It was badly needed by the mother church in Phoenix, because a recent drought had the people living in hard times. Some of the Caldwellians were so enraged that they seized Pablo and dragged him into the streets. It seems to be a bad plan to come between people and their money. The Caldwellians were threatening to kill Pablo, when Pedro made an appearance. He was no longer in charge, but seemed to be enjoying the troubles Pedro was having. One would think that two pillars of the Caldwellian movement could overcome their differences, but all Pedro could think about was that Pablo was getting his comeuppance. After all, he had dragged Caldwellians to jail, so maybe this was his due reward.

Meanwhile, the new marshal, after Marshal Garfias' untimely death, heard the uproar. Immediately he brought some deputies with him and they stopped the yelling. They arrested Pablo and ordered him to be bound around his feet and hands with his own belt, just as the prophet in Tucson had said. The marshal then inquired what the problem was, and some in the crowd shouted one thing, and some another. The mob started getting unruly again, so the marshal fired a shot in the air to get their attention. The same shouting ensued, and as he could not learn the facts because of the uproar, the marshal ordered Pablo to be brought into the barracks. The violence of the mob was so great that he had to be carried by the deputies. The crowd that followed kept shouting, 'Away with him!'" Seems money was quite important to more than just the Caldwellians.

# The Value of the Diamond

Just as Pablo was about to be brought into the barracks, he asked if he could address the crowd. He noticed there was a great variety of people: Catholics, Methodists, nonbelievers, townsfolk, and some Caldwellians. The marshal turned down his request, but Pablo suggested the crowd would calm down. The marshal said, "Okay, we'll give it a try, as long as it works." Pablo went to the steps, bound, and accompanied by deputies. He nodded his head to the people for silence, and there was a great hush, so the marshal motioned for him to proceed.

He said, "I am a Mexican American."

Immediately someone in the crowd yelled, "Go back where you came from!"

Pablo went on to explain that he was "born in San Jose, California, and moved to Jerome before coming here to Phoenix. My Catholic upbringing was at the Basilica of St. Joseph where I learned much about the Scriptures. I was injured as a youth, which I call the 'thorn in my flesh,' and prayed for healing, which still has not come."

"And no divine help is coming your way today, either!" yelled an angry man.

"I persecuted the new movement of Caldwellians," continued Pablo, "for being the bearers of fake news. They claimed to do healings and said strange things about life and death. They even offered baptism as a way to die to the old life and take on the new life they were offering. I was given permission from Marshal Garfias to persecute Caldwellians in Tucson, and I went there to bring them back to Phoenix for punishment. While I was on my way and approaching Tucson, about noon a great light from heaven suddenly shone about me."

Someone yelled, "Yeah, it's called the sun!"

# The Value of the Diamond

Most didn't laugh because they wanted to hear the story, so Pablo continued. "I fell to the ground and heard a voice saying to me, 'Pablo, Pablo, why are you persecuting me?' I answered, 'Who are you, Lord?' Then he said to me, 'I am Jim Caldwell of Prescott whom you are persecuting.' Now those who were with me saw the light but did not hear the voice of the one who was speaking to me." The crowd was quiet now and listening. "I asked, 'What am I to do, Lord?' The Lord said to me, 'Get up and go to Tucson; there you will be told everything that has been assigned to you to do.' Since I could not see because of the brightness of that light, those who were with me led me to Tucson.

"A certain Jesse, who was a devout man according to the law and well-spoken of by all the Catholics living there, came to me; and standing beside me, he said, 'Brother Pablo, regain your sight!' In that very hour I regained my sight and saw him. Then he said, 'The God of our ancestors has chosen you to know his will, to see the Righteous One and to hear his own voice; for you will be his witness to all the world of what you have seen and heard. And now why do you delay? Get up, be baptized, and have your sins washed away, calling on his name.'"

"What's this got to do with losing our money?" asked a member of the Caldwellians.

Pablo just continued, "After I had returned to Phoenix and while I was praying in the church, I fell into a trance and saw Jim saying to me, 'Hurry and get out of Phoenix quickly, because they will not accept your testimony about me.' And I said, 'Lord, they themselves know that in every church I imprisoned and beat those who believed in you. And while the blood of your first witness Jack was shed, I myself was standing by, approving and keeping the coats of those who killed him.' Then he said to me, 'Go for I will send you far away to Utah, Colorado, New Mexico, and all over Mexico itself.'"

Up to this point, most of the people in the crowd listened to him, but then they shouted, "Away with this guy. He's just trying to save his own skin!"

The deputies brought him into the barracks and had him flogged, to find out why there was such an outcry against him. Discovering that this was a religious problem about money, they took him to the Catholics and had him stand before them. Pablo said, "Brothers, up to this day I have lived my life with a clear conscience before God." The Catholic priest in charge ordered those standing near him to strike him on the mouth. At this, Pablo said to him, "God will strike you, you dying saguaro cactus!"

Those standing nearby said, "Do you dare to insult God's priest?"

Pablo focused them, saying, "I am on trial for stealing money that I did not steal!"

Then a great clamor arose and some stood up and said, "We find nothing wrong with this man. Besides, the problem is with his fellow Caldwellians."

When the troubles became violent, the deputies took Pablo by force and brought him back to the barracks. That night the Lord stood near him and said, "Keep up your courage! For just as you have testified for me in Phoenix, so you must bear witness also in San Francisco."

In the morning, the Catholics and many others joined in a conspiracy and bound themselves by an oath, "neither to eat nor drink until they had killed Pablo." They went to the marshal and said, "We have strictly bound ourselves by an oath to eat nothing until we have killed Pablo. Now then, you must bring him to our bishop on the pretext that you want to make a more thorough examination of his case. And we are ready to do away with him before he arrives."

Now a Caldwellian heard about the ambush; so he went to the barracks and told Pablo. After that, he went to the marshal and also told him about the ambush. He said, "Do not be persuaded by them, for more than forty of their men are lying in ambush for him." The marshal summoned two of his deputies and said, "Get ready to leave by nine o'clock tonight for Wickenburg with forty men." He also told them to have a horse for Pablo to ride and take him safely to the governor. Then he wrote a letter to be handed to the governor that said:

"Greetings, Governor Irwin,

This man was seized by the Catholics and others and was about to be killed by them, but then I came with some deputies and rescued him. Since I wanted to know the charge for which they accused him, I had him brought to their bishop. I found that he was accused concerning questions of money for church purposes, but was charged with nothing deserving death or imprisonment. When I was informed that there would be a plot against the man, I sent him to you at once."

With appreciation for your help,
Marshal Wilcox

So Pablo was taken to the governor under the cover of night. When they came to Wickenburg and delivered the letter

# The Value of the Diamond

to the governor, they presented Pablo also before him. On reading the letter, he said, "I will give you a hearing when your accusers arrive. Then he ordered that he be kept under guard. Five days later the Catholic bishop arrived, along with a representative of the Caldwellians. When Pablo had been summoned, an attorney for the Catholics began to speak. "Governor, we appreciate all you have done to help our Arizona Territory, but to detain you no further, I beg you to hear us briefly. We have, in fact, found this man a pestilent fellow, an agitator among all the Catholics throughout America and Mexico, and a ringleader of the sect of Caldwellians. By examining him yourself you will be able to learn from him concerning everything of which we accuse him."

The governor said, "And what about the representative of the Caldwellians? Come and share what you accuse this man of doing." Nothing happened at first, so the governor was obviously getting frustrated, then before he could complain the crowd separated. Both Pablo and the governor were squinting to try to see who was coming forward. As he approached, Pablo's jaw dropped. Of all the people it could be, it turned out to be none other than Pedro. Pablo's blood coursed red hot through his body, and all he wanted to do was break his chains and wrapt them around Pedro's neck. The two men stared at one another for a long time, while the crowd experienced an awkward silence.

The governor finally said, "I don't have all day, speak now or I'll have you jailed, too."

"Your honor," Pedro said in a rather halting voice, "all I can say is that the man standing next to you was charged by the Caldwellians to collect an offering from the churches in Mexico, to help us in Phoenix. He accomplished this task, which we greatly appreciated, but when he arrived, he didn't turn over the money."

Then the governor motioned for Pablo to speak, and he said, "I cheerfully make my defense, first to the Catholics. They did not find me disputing with anyone in their church, nor stirring up a crowd. Neither can they prove to you the charge that they now bring against me. As far as the second charge, according to the Caldwellians, I stole the money collected for the Caldwellian church of Phoenix. It is true that the money made it across the border with my bodyguard Chuy, but it is not true that I stole it. We have reason to believe Chuy returned with the money to Mexico."

"Who do you mean," questioned the governor, "when you say we?" At that point, Francisco, Jasper, and Rose were in the crowd and raised their hands, so the governor motioned for Pablo to continue.

"I do my best always to have a clear conscience toward God and all people." But the governor, who was rather well informed about the Caldwellians, decided to adjourn the hearing by saying, "I will decide your case in the next few days," then ordered Pablo to be kept in custody.

Several days later, Governor Irwin brought his Catholic wife to hear Pablo speak concerning faith in Jim Caldwell. And as he discussed justice, self-control, and the coming judgment, the governor became frightened and said, "You need to leave. I will send for you again later." At the same time the governor hoped that the money collected by Pablo would show up and prove Pablo's innocence. For that reason, the governor sent for him on numerous occasions and conversed with him. After two years had passed, Governor Irwin resigned his position and President Benjamin Harrison appointed Oakes Murphy as the successor.

Three days after Governor Murphy arrived in the territory, he went from Wickenburg to Phoenix where the bishop gave him a report against Pablo. Then the bishop requested, as a favor to himself, to have Pablo transferred to Phoenix. The governor replied that Pablo would remain in Wickenburg, but they could travel back there with him, and "if there is anything wrong about the man, let him be accused." When they returned, the governor took his seat and ordered Pablo to be brought out.

Several Catholics made the trip to Wickenburg, and brought serious charges of theft against him, which they could not prove. Pablo simply denied all charges, but the new governor wanted to do the Catholics a favor. He asked Pablo, "Do you wish to go to Phoenix and be tried there by me on these charges?" Pablo said, "I have done no wrong to the Catholics, as you very well know, so I request to see President Harrison." The new governor replied, "You want to appeal to the President?" then with a laugh he said, "To the President you will go."

President Harrison enjoyed promoting the Transcontinental Railroad, by taking occasional trips across the country to San Francisco. Governor Murphy decided to send Pablo to San Francisco in hopes of gaining audience with the President at some point. It was at the train station that the three faithful companions from his Mexico trip said their goodbyes. Francisco was going back to Mexico, while Jasper planned to return to Flagstaff. Rose decided to reclaim her ministry in Tucson, but all four had tears in their eyes as the train embarked for Los Angeles.

Pablo was accompanied by a deputy, who thoughtfully told Pablo that if he hadn't appealed to the President, he probably

# The Value of the Diamond

Would have been set free, but at least he was deemed to not be a risk. As the train lumbered down the newly laid tracks, Pablo had a nice view looking south. As he stared out at the majestic South Mountain, he couldn't help but remember the risen Lord saying, "You will be my witness in Phoenix, and the Arizona Territory, and to the ends of the earth." He thought that San Francisco must surely be what Jim Caldwell meant by the end of the earth. Pablo started falling asleep as he noticed the Gila Bend Mountains on his right. It helped that it was hot out in the desert, making him want to sleep, as the train continued clacking down the track in a rhythmic pattern. Even the deputy was comfortable that Pablo was no danger, so he too fell asleep. This lonely stretch of train track slowly brought them to across the punishing desert to Yuma, where they stopped at the depot.

Founded in 1873, Yuma quickly became known as a stopover place for immigrants heading for the California gold fields. A rough collection of outcasts quickly caused the crime rate to surge, and in 1875 the town built the Yuma Territorial Prison. As Pablo and the deputy got off to stretch for a bit, the deputy pointed at the prison and said, "Pablo, you sure you want to live out the rest of your life in a place like that?" Pablo was sure about his innocence, so he brushed off the comment. Meanwhile, the engineer got word that a bad dust storm was raging across the desert between Yuma and Los Angeles.

Pablo said to the engineer, "I can see that the trip will be dangerous and with heavy loss, to the train and also our lives."

But the engineer paid no attention to Pablo saying, "We made it here from Phoenix and we'll make it to Los Angeles."

"All aboard!" the conductor barked a few minutes later.

A moderate south wind began to blow, but the engineer still

believed they could achieve their purpose. As they made their way northwest of Yuma, the winds slowly became more violent and the engineer asked for assistance from the conductor.

"A dust storm is kicking up," announced the engineer, "and I can barely see. Are we getting close to Lake Cahuilla?"

"Sorry sir," replied the conductor. "I lost sense of where we were quite a while ago."

The winds were so strong that the desert sand felt like sandpaper scraping across the face. The engineer reluctantly slowed down, then a powerful thud was heard and the train slowed to a stop.

"What happened?" screamed someone on board, while others fell out of their seats.

"We're gonna' die out in this desert!" yelled another.

As many passengers were getting up to see what was going on, the conductor walked hurriedly through the cars and cautioned everyone to stay in place. He said, "You might not find your way back on board due to the dust storm, so sit down!" By the time he got up to the locomotive, the engineer had struggled to the front and found the problem. As the winds howled, they had a hard time hearing one another, but soon enough the engineer said, "We ran into a herd of cattle standing on the tracks."

They were stranded there for several anxious days. The nights were even worse as the coyotes gathered to devour an evening's dinner of freshly killed beef. Each day people helped as they could to remove the dead carcasses from the tracks, and even Pablo did his fair share of work. The people had been without food for a long time when Pablo said to the engineer, "You should have listened to me, but I urge you now to keep up your courage, for there will be no loss of life among us."

# The Value of the Diamond

"How do you figure?" he asked.

Pablo responded, "Last night an angel stood by me and said, 'Do not be afraid, Pablo. You must stand before the President, and God has granted safety to all those who are traveling with you.' So keep up your courage, for I have faith in God that it will be exactly as I have been told." The engineer shook his head back and forth and went back to work.

Just before daybreak, Pablo spoke to his fellow passengers, urging all of them to take some food, saying "It's been a long time that we have been without food, having eaten nothing. I urge you to take some food from the dining car. It will help you survive." After he had said this, he took bread; and giving thanks to God in the presence of all, he broke it and began to eat. Then all of them were encouraged and took food for themselves.

Once they were finally ready to travel again, the conductor told everyone to take their seats. The train lurched forward and crossed the bloody tracks, and they were at last on their way. When the Southern Pacific train pulled into the Los Angeles station, the passengers were greeted with unusual kindness. Since it had begun to rain and was cold, the station workers kindled a fire and welcomed everyone. Pablo had gathered a bundle of brushwood and was putting it on the fire, when a Mojave rattler bit him. When the people saw what happened, they were perplexed at his calmness. They were expecting him to swell up or drop dead, but after they had waited a long time and saw that nothing unusual happened to him, they changed their minds. And the deputy even felt stronger about the goodness and innocence of Pablo.

The final leg of the journey went smooth, and the train chugged into the San Francisco depot. Pablo was then told that he would be allowed to live by himself, with the deputy who was guarding him. Three days later he called together the local leaders of the Catholics and said, "Though I was arrested in Phoenix and handed over to the authorities here in San Francisco, they wanted to release me because there was no reason for the death penalty in my case." But when the Catholics objected, because they complained that Pablo stole money and spread fake news about the resurrection of Jim Caldwell, he was compelled to appeal to the President. The authorities replied, "We have received no letters from Phoenix about you, and no one here has said anything evil about you. But we would like to hear from you what you think, for with regard to the Caldwellians we know that everywhere it is spoken against."

After they had a set day to meet with him, they came to him at his lodging in great numbers. From morning to evening, Pablo explained the matter to them, testifying to the kingdom of God and trying to convince them about Jim Caldwell. Some were convinced by what he said, while others refused to believe. He lived there two whole years, supported by offerings from local Caldwellians. He welcomed all who came to him, proclaiming the kingdom of God and teaching about the Jim Caldwell with all boldness and without hindrance. By the way, President Harrison never made it to San Francisco.

## SCENE TWO
San Francisco

P ablo's house arrest was in a meager home in view of the Emporium, which not only housed a department store but the Supreme Court. The deputy who was in charge of Pablo since Phoenix, remained loyal to his task and even became a believer. One day, Pablo got a telegram from a local Caldwellian congregation. They had questions, and having heard that Pablo and Pedro were at odds, they didn't bother to mention it was Pedro who was their founder. Here are their questions:

---

DEAR PABLO,

HOW DO GRACE AND SALVATION GO
    TOGETHER?
HOW DO FAITH AND RIGHTEOUSNESS GO
    TOGETHER?
PLEASE TALK ABOUT JUSTIFICATION.
HOW CAN JEWS BE SAVED?
WHAT IS THE NEW LIFE IN JIM?

AFFECTIONATELY,
THE CALDWELLIAN CHURCH OF SAN FRANCISCO

---

Pablo didn't have to think very long before starting his response. He'd been thinking about these issues for a long time now, and he was feeling pretty good about the clarity he had come to since beginning his ministry. So, here's how he wrote his opening salutation.

"Pablo, a servant of Jim Caldwell, called to be an apostle, set apart for the gospel of God, which he promised beforehand through his prophets in the Holy Scriptures, the gospel concerning Jim Caldwell, who was descended from an Aztec King according to the flesh, and was declared to be the Son of God by resurrection from the dead." Pablo stopped for a moment, and hoped those last few words would sink in.

He had heard way too much about Jim Caldwell being God on earth. Jim was not. He was born a human and died a human. It was the power of the resurrection that made him the Son of God. Getting that off his chest, he continued with his salutation. "It was Jim Caldwell, through whom we have received grace and apostleship to bring about the obedience of faith among all the unbelievers for the sake of his name, including yourselves who are called to belong to Jim Caldwell.

"To all God's beloved in San Francisco, who are called to be saints:

"Grace to you and peace from God our Father and Jim Caldwell."

Pablo was delighted with his salutation, and he was now ready to hit them hot and heavy, like a tortilla fresh from the fire, with his thoughts about God. "For I am not ashamed of the gospel; it is the power of God for salvation to everyone who has faith, to the Jew first and also to the unbelievers. For in it the righteousness of God is revealed through faith for faith; as it is written, 'The one who is righteous will live by faith.'" Again Pablo smiled. He was tired of hearing people speak poorly of the Jews. Don't people understand that everything started with God choosing the Jews out of all the races on earth? How could anyone in their right mind speak against them? They are automatically included. It is the rest of us who seek inclusion.

Pablo paused and thought that this house arrest business was doing just fine for him. He then looked at the telegram and was more than ready to tackle these great questions. First was, "How do grace and salvation go together?" His Road to Tucson experience powerfully told him that God doesn't impart salvation by way of what we do, but what God does. Pablo used the Jews as an example: "Now we know that whatever the law says, it speaks to those who are under the law, so that every mouth may be silenced, and the whole world may be held accountable to God. For 'no human being will be justified in his sight' by deeds prescribed by the law, for through the law comes the knowledge of sin." He then thought that was a bit too heavy. He wasn't going to change it, but maybe answering the next question would help to make it easier to understand.

"How do faith and righteousness go together?" Pablo wanted the people from the Caldwellian Church of San Francisco to know that righteousness comes through faith, so here is what he said: "But now, apart from law, the righteousness of God has been disclosed, and is attested by the law and the prophets, the righteousness of God through faith in Jim Caldwell for all who believe. For there is no distinction, since all have sinned and fall short of the glory of God." Pablo still feared he was being too heavy with his explanations, so he stopped and prayed that God would give him a practical answer about human faith and divine righteousness. Pablo muttered a thanks to the Lord when he got what he was looking for in the person of Aapo.

He wrote, "If Aapo was justified by works, he has something to boast about, but not before God. For what does the scripture say? 'Aapo believed God, and it was reckoned to him as righteousness.'" How could Aapo be good before the law was even given? Pablo hoped and prayed that people would catch this all important point, then continued with, "Therefore his faith 'was reckoned to him as righteousness.' Now the words, 'it was reckoned to him,' were written not for his sake alone, but for ours also. It will be reckoned to us who believe in him who raised Jim Caldwell from the dead, who was handed over to death for our sins and was raised for our justification." That played well into the next item on the telegram, "Talk about justification."

This was important. Pablo wanted his readers to catch the fact that through the death and resurrection of Jim Caldwell, they are justified. All they need to do is take that blind leap of faith, just as he did. So he wrote, "Since we are justified by faith," Pablo desperately hoped they would get it that the action was completed, "we have peace with God." In other words, we are made right with God, so have confidence. Does that make everything good? He continued, "And not only that, but we also boast in our sufferings, knowing that suffering produces endurance, and endurance produces character, and character produces hope, and hope does not disappoint us, because God's love has been poured into our hearts through the Holy Spirit that has been given to us."

Pablo knew justification was a huge concept, so he wrote, "But God proves his love for us in that while we still were sinners Jim died for us." He then suggested that Adam was a type of Jim: "Death exercised dominion from Adam to Abund, even over those whose sins were not like the transgression of Adam, who is a type of the one who was to come." He explained that the free gift "is not like the trespass. For if the many died through the one man's trespass, much more surely have the grace of God and the free gift in the grace of the one man, Jim Caldwell, abounded for the many."

Pablo wasn't happy with the smoothness of his argument, so he said, "Therefore just as one man's trespass led to condemnation for all, so one man's act of righteousness leads to justification and life for all." He stopped and prayed that the readers would understand this point. In his mind, it was abundantly obvious that the one man's trespass was Adam that leads to condemnation. And if Jim was anything like Adam, then Jim's act of righteousness likewise leads to justification. They are polar opposites. He then wondered which path people would prefer to take if they only understood.

He wanted to make his point crystal clear, so he continued, "But law came in, with the result that sin multiplied." He desperately hoped people would not stop reading, because his point was next. "But where sin increased, grace abounded all the more." A bad thought crossed his mind, so he wrote, "Should we continue in sin in order that grace may abound? By no means! How can we who died to sin go on living in it? Do you not know that all of us who have been baptized into Jim were baptized into his death? We have been buried with him by baptism into death, so that, just as Jim was raised from the dead by the glory of the Father, so we too might walk in newness of life."

He thought for a moment that his argument might sound like grace could cancel moral obligations, so he wrote, "What then? Should we sin because we are not under law but under grace? By no means!" Pablo felt a twinge of anger at the very thought that freedom from law could give permission to sin. He explained that it takes obedience from the heart. To put it plainly, he wrote, "Because it is sin that leads to death, then the free gift of God is eternal life in Jim." He had one more concern that justification by faith might seem to equate the law with sin. Here's how he dealt with that: "What then should we say? That the law is sin? By no means! Yet if it had not been for the law, I would not have known sin, and the very commandment that promised life proved to be death to me. So the law is holy, and the commandment is holy and just and good."

That was a lot to think about concerning justification, so Pablo wrote a quick summary thought: "Did what is good, then, bring death to me? By no means! It was sin, working death in me through what is good, in order that sin might be shown to be sin, and through the commandment might become sinful beyond measure." Okay, Pablo was done with that. He was exhausted. He thought that it was surely divine inspiration, because he barely understood what he was writing. He called his deputy friend in and read it to him to see what he thought

"Pretty heavy stuff, I'd say," the deputy responded. "But at least it will give people plenty of food for thought!"

Pablo agreed, and then was ready to move on to a positive note. "There is therefore now no condemnation for those who are in Jim Caldwell. For the law of the spirit of life in Jim has set you free from the law of sin and death." He also wanted them to know that the Holy Spirit was the spirit of Jim, so he said, "Anyone who does not have the Spirit of Jim does not belong to him. But if Jim is in you, though the body is dead because of sin, the Spirit is life because of righteousness."

He also shared that the world, and everything in it, awaits redemption. "I consider that the sufferings of this present time are not worth comparing with the glory about to be revealed to us. For the world waits with eager longing for the revealing of

# The Value of the Diamond

the children of God. We know that the whole creation has been groaning in labor pains until now; and not only the creation, but we ourselves, who have the first fruits of the Spirit, groan inwardly while we wait for adoption, the redemption of our bodies." He then encouraged them to be hopeful and to let the Spirit guide prayer, "with sighs too deep for words." Pablo felt that Spirit, and tried to put it into some sort of poetry.

> We know that all things
> work together for good,
> for those who love God,
> who are called
> according to his purpose."

Pablo really liked the way he had answered their request to talk about justification. He closed it out with some assurances, like, "Oh, what can I say? If God is for us, who is against us? It is God who justifies. Who is to condemn? It is Jim Caldwell, who died, yes, who was raised, who with God, who indeed intercedes for us. Who will separate us from the love of Jim? Will hardship, or distress, or persecution, or famine, or nakedness, or peril, or sword? No, in all these things we are more than conquerors through him who loved us." Again he smiled as the words just flowed, "There is nothing that will ever change my mind. Whether in this life or the next. Not heavenly beings, marshals, things that haunt our past, present circumstances, nor whatever tomorrow brings. From the San Francisco peaks to the depths of Death Valley, nor anything else in all creation, will be able to separate us from the love of God in Jim Caldwell."

He was so excited about what he just wrote, that he called

for his deputy again. Since he was now a believer, he wanted to run that last bit by him. The deputy sat at his feet with attentive ears. As Pablo read that last paragraph back to him, the deputy raised his hands in celebration and said, "You are a testimony of the truth you just wrote. Neither the threat of death nor the taking of freedom can stop you. Not the Catholic bishops, nor the governor of Arizona, nor the President of the United States, because the love of God dwells inside you by the power of the Spirit of Jim Caldwell."

Pablo sensed a peace that passes all understanding, from the testimony of the deputy, but just now he was feeling a bit tired. The problem was that he was on a roll, so Pablo looked at the next question. How can Jews be saved? He started to write, "I am speaking the truth in Jim—I am not lying; my conscience confirms it by the Holy Spirit—I have great sorrow and unceasing anguish in my heart." He really was too tired to continue the letter, so he just put down his pen and paper and went to sleep.

The next morning he was refreshed and ready to tackle the last question. He wrote that not all Jews were saved in the first place. After all, God's choosing of a group of people was out of God's mercy and compassion. Pablo felt some frustration for the Jews, so next he wrote, "Nothing said they were required to participate in their election as God's people." He thought for a moment that people shouldn't even try to figure this all out, because we can understand God about as well as an ant can comprehend a human.

Pablo was feeling a need to cite scripture, to get himself on solid ground. He then noted the prophet Isaiah who said, "Though the number of the children of Israel were like the sand of the sea, only a remnant of them will be saved." He then wrote that unbelieving Jews have rejected the gospel, because they did not strive for it on the basis of faith. He again quoted a text from Isaiah with, "See, I am laying in Zion a stone that will make people stumble, a rock that will make them fall, and whoever believes in him will not be put to shame."

He explained that the problem was that they sought to establish their own righteousness by way of law. What they didn't get was that the law leads to Jim. The law was meant to bring life, but now wholeness comes from believing that God raised Jim from the dead. Pablo then thought, it's all okay. Disbelief creates opportunity for non-Jews to receive the gospel. Then he wrote: "I ask then, has God rejected his people? By no means! God has not rejected his people." Pablo frowned for a moment when he realized that it wasn't about God rejecting the Jews, it was intolerant human beings looking for opportunities to discard people who aren't like them.

He noted a story from the book of Kings, then wrote, "At the present time there is a remnant, chosen by grace. But if it is by grace, it is no longer on the basis of works, otherwise grace would no longer be grace." He explained that even if Israel failed to obtain God's grace, the "elect obtained it, but the rest were hardened." He further noted that it didn't mean the hardened were lost forever because they would become envious of non-Jews and be incited to receive salvation. His point was to always hold out hope that all people would sooner or later fall into the arms of God's grace.

Pablo was again feeling pretty good about the letter. Next he noted that not all Jewish people are Jews, because a person can be Jewish by race but not by religion. He then made the analogy of an olive tree, where Jews and non-Jews are branches. Some Jews become broken off from the tree while some non-Jews become grafted in. Then he cautioned the non-Jews about boasting, "Do not boast over the branches. If you do boast, remember that it is not you that support the root, but the root that supports you." He further cautioned the non-Jews, that, "if God did not spare the natural branches, perhaps he will not spare you." Pablo wanted to give some hope, so he finally mentioned that all believers in Jim Caldwell will be saved, whether they are Jews or non-Jews.

Pablo sat back in his chair and felt proud of what he had just sketched out, until he wryly smiled for remembering that he, too, should be careful about boasting. He then climbed into his bed and fell hard asleep. As soon as he woke up, he turned back to the telegram and read the final question: "What is the new life in Jim?" A holy smile broke across his faith because this is what he really wanted to talk about all along. Here's how he started: "I beg of you therefore, brothers and sisters, by the mercies of God, to present your bodies as a living sacrifice, holy and acceptable to God, which is your spiritual worship. Do not be conformed to this world, but be transformed by the renewing of your minds, so that you may discern the will of God—what is good and acceptable and perfect."

He then wanted to talk about the new life in Jim with respect to community, so he wrote, "Let love be genuine; hate what is evil, hold fast to what is good; love one another with mutual affection; outdo one another in showing honor. Do not lack in zeal, be ardent in spirit, serve the Lord. Rejoice in hope, be patient in suffering, persevere in prayer. Contribute to the needs of the saints; extend hospitality to strangers." Knowing the challenge of being a Caldwellian, he wrote, "Bless those who persecute you; bless and do not curse them. Rejoice with those who rejoice, weep with those who weep. Live in harmony with one another; do not be haughty, but associate with the lowly; do not claim to be wiser than you are. Do not repay anyone evil for evil, but take thought for what is noble in the sight of all."

This last bit of writing about the practical application of his heavy thinking struck a frustrating chord in his heart. He believed every word he wrote, but he couldn't shake the thought of Pedro out of his mind. Their struggle over authority served no purpose in the Caldwellian kingdom, but all he could think was that Pedro started it. If Pedro hadn't been so haughty about being an original follower of Jim's, the problems would never have begun. Then a new blinding light hit him in the form of a question. In some ways it was more transformational than the one on the road to Tucson.

Why couldn't he acknowledge the power of his own transformation by the risen Lord? Did that moment back then make no difference? He reeled in pain, because it was the first time he was ever able to admit his ego problem. He felt truly struck down. All of a sudden the words of Jim Caldwell made sense to him for the very first time: "Follow me." In others words, it wasn't about himself. He needed to put away his ego if he were to truly follow the leading's of the Holy Spirit. He stopped for a long bit of prayer, and finally realized he had to forgive Pedro, even though Pedro wasn't asking for forgiveness. Somehow the pain just drained from him, and after a little more time he was ready to get back to writing.

Pablo was truly excited for the Caldwellian community in San Francisco. Having deep affection for people he never even met, he continued, "If it is possible, so far as it depends on you, live peaceably with all. Beloved, never avenge yourselves, but leave room for the justice of God; for it is written, 'Vengeance is mine, I will repay, says the Lord.' No, 'if your enemies are hungry, feed them; if they are thirsty, give them something to drink; for by doing this you will heap burning coals on their heads.' Do not be overcome by evil, but overcome evil with good." Pablo stopped for a moment and thought about the Russians hanging Jim Caldwell. All of a sudden it crossed his mind that Jim was not overcome by the Russians, but overcame them with the resurrection.

He then exhorted them to be subject to governing authorities. He actually felt good about his witness of being subject to house arrest. It was something he could easily defy by simply walking away, but he was putting his life in the hands of God by deferring to the powers that be. Then he decided to address another problem. He told them to pay taxes, saying, "Pay to all what is due them—taxes to whom taxes are due, revenue to whom revenue is due, respect to whom respect is due, honor to whom honor is due."

The words were still flowing, so Pablo added, "Owe no one anything, except to love one another; for the one who loves another has fulfilled the law." He explained that the law can be summed up with, "Love your neighbor as yourself. Love does no wrong to a neighbor; therefore, love is the fulfilling of the law." He urged them that "salvation is nearer to us now than when we became believers," and that we should "put on the spirit of Jim Caldwell." Pablo then exhorted them about the problem of judgment, asking "Why do you pass judgment on your brother or sister? Or you, why do you despise your brother or sister? For we all stand before the judgment seat of God."

That felt right, but Pablo was ready for a break. He stepped out on the front porch where he was loosely being held captive, and did a little street preaching. The city folk seemed busy and showed no interest in his thoughts. He had more to say, but decided to put it to use in his letter. He went back in and started writing. "Let us therefore no longer pass judgment on one another, but resolve instead never to put a stumbling block or hindrance in the way of another."

He explained that the "kingdom of God is not food and drink but righteousness and peace and joy in the Holy Spirit. Let us then pursue what makes for peace and for mutual upbuilding, for whatever does not proceed from faith is sin." He then asked that God would "grant you to live in harmony with one another, in accordance with Jim Caldwell, so that together you may with one voice glorify the God and Father of our Lord." The he said, "May the God of hope fill you with all joy and peace in believing, so that you may abound in hope by the power of the Holy Spirit."

Pablo was filled with satisfaction as he realized he was finished responding to the telegram, yet he sensed, as usual, that he needed to say a bit more. He appended, "I myself feel confident about you, my brothers and sisters, that you yourselves are full of goodness, filled with all knowledge, and able to instruct one another." Almost as a sense of excuse, he gave some reasons why his letter to them was written so boldly, then he shared a quote from the prophet Isaiah. He felt bad that he was under arrest, so he wrote, "I do hope to see you on my journey and to be sent on by you, once I have enjoyed your company for a little while." He finished with the comment that "by God's will I will come to you with joy and be refreshed in your company. The God of peace be with all of you. Amen."

That felt better, but first he wanted to dole out some thank yous. He told them to pray for Rose and Big Nose Kate, "who worked with me in the name of Jim Caldwell, and who risked their necks for my life, to whom not only I give thanks, but also to all the churches." He then listed twenty-nine individuals, of which one-third were women. It was important to him to celebrate women, because Jim Caldwell was ahead of his time in teaching equality. Next, he paused for a moment and remembered how Elena and Carlos quite literally put their lives on the line for his sake during the riot in Mexico City. He once again finished by saying to, "Greet one another with a holy kiss. All the Caldwellian churches greet you."

Pablo didn't seem to want to end this letter. It turned out to be the longest one and carried the depths of his thought since the road to Tucson. All of a sudden he felt a need to add an extra warning. "I urge you, brothers and sisters, to keep an eye on those who cause dissensions and offenses, in opposition to the teaching that you have learned; avoid them." That warning came from his direct experience with the challenges of starting Caldwellian churches. He then added, "For such people do not serve our Lord, but their own appetites, and by smooth talk and flattery they deceive the hearts of the simple-minded." No little bit of frustration welled up inside him, so he added even more. "For while your obedience is known to all, so that I rejoice over you, I want you to be wise in what is good, and guileless in what is evil. The grace of Jim Caldwell be with you."

He really and truly didn't want to end this letter, because he knew it might be his last. He decided it was time to sign off with a doxology. "Now to God who is able to strengthen you according to my gospel and the proclamation of Jim Caldwell, according to the revelation of the mystery that was kept secret for long ages but is now disclosed, and through the prophetic writings is made known to all, according to the command of the eternal God, to bring about the obedience of faith—to the only wise God, through Jim Caldwell, to whom be the glory forever! Amen."

# The Value of the Diamond

Pablo then folded the letter and spent some time praying over it. Something told him he would never get to visit that wonderful church in San Francisco, and his heart broke a little. He also heard some stories while in prison, as one does, about Pedro. It came to his attention that Pedro was the one who founded the Caldwellian Church of San Francisco. He knew it was wrong, but he smiled just a little bit about the fact that the people were asking their questions of him rather than of Pedro. He also heard that Pedro was about to be arrested in San Francisco and was probably going to be sentenced to this very same jail of sorts. His last prayer was, "Please Lord, don't let Pedro be my roommate."

## EPILOGUE
### Angel Island

As so often are the intriguing ways of God, Pedro got in trouble in San Francisco. To Pablo's utter despair, Pedro was sentenced to house arrest and, sure enough, became his roommate. To say they got along would be as likely as a golden eagle getting along with a rattlesnake. They argued loudly day and night until neighbors requested something be done about it. The authorities decided to send Pablo to Angel Island, the largest island in California's San Francisco Bay. In 1850, President Millard Fillmore declared the island a military reserve and during the Civil War, the island was fortified.

Pablo arrived and settled into his jail cell, and very soon he got word that Rose had left Tucson and was one her way to visit him. Well, not just him. The mother church in Phoenix commissioned her to visit both Pablo and Pedro. When she arrived, she discovered that Pablo had been moved to Angel Island, so she first settled into a room being supplied by the Caldwellian Church of San Francisco. The next day she found the house where Pedro was at, and was surprised to find Pablo's deputy staying there to keep official watch over Pedro.

Rose asked the deputy, "Why didn't you return to Phoenix after Pablo was moved to Angel Island? After all, you couldn't offer your services there."

The deputy said, "I have become a Caldwellian, and I have joined the Caldwellian Church of San Francisco. It has become my mission now to provide watch over Pedro."

Pedro said, "I thought you were here to see me!" They all three smiled and Rose gave Pedro and hug. They sat down and had a long and wonderful visit, but Rose was anxious to get on to see Pablo. They had traveled so much together through America and Mexico, and now she was concerned about his safety at Angel Island. She said her goodbyes, then went there next. The boat trip to the island was quite hazardous, with choppy waters and plenty of sharks. It took a while to gain entrance as a visitor, but before long she got through the red tape and saw him. He was brought to a small, rather chilly room, and they could only sit at a desk across from one another. It didn't matter. They both were overjoyed and praised God. After another great visit, Rose left for her room at the church, promising to return each day.

———

That night Pablo received a mesage from Jim. It was to give comfort to fellow believers that Jim Caldwell was already with his people through the power of the Holy Spirit. The experience woke him up, so he wrote it down. Here's the first of seven messages that Jim Caldwell wanted to share through Pablo, and this one was to the church in Mexico City. It wasn't just for that church either. It simply represented situations in many of the churches.

*The first message—to Mexico City, Mexico*

"I know your works, your toil and your patient endurance. I know that you cannot tolerate evildoers; you have tested those who claim to be apostles but are not, and have found them to be false. I also know that you are enduring patiently and bearing up for the sake of my name, and that you have not grown weary. But I have this against you that you have abandoned the love you had at first. Remember then from what you have fallen; repent, and do the works you did at first. If not, I will come to you and remove your lamp from its place, unless you repent. Yet this is to your credit: you hate the works of the false missionaries, which I also hate. Let anyone who has an ear listen to what the Spirit is saying to the churches. To everyone who conquers, I will give permission to eat from the tree of life that is in the paradise of God." Then Pablo decided to summarize, because he really did like getting in the last word:

Your virtue is patient endurance.
Your vice is abandoning previous works of love.
My advice is to repent or lose the Holy Spirit.

———

Pablo was a bit cautious after this somewhat troubling message, so he sat back to relax in his makeshift cell. He was about to fall asleep when he received a vision, or maybe it was a dream, he couldn't tell. Whatever happened, he looked up and saw a door to heaven standing open. At first he thought he had died, but then he heard a voice saying, "Come up here, and I will show you what must take place after this." Still not sure if the voice was talking about himself or what, he soon sensed he was there in the spirit. As Pablo looked around, he saw things that he was simply incapable of describing. Finally, he saw a rainbow and thought at least that was familiar.

The next day Rose showed up for her visit, and Pablo was

happy to have someone to talk to. First thing he did was hand the letter to Rose and asked her to get it to their friends in Mexico City in whatever way she could. Next he told her about the dream.

"You went to heaven last night?" exclaimed a wide-eyed Rose.

Pablo said, "I have no idea, but I think I was there in the spirit."

Being very hesitant at first, Rose finally asked, "What was it like?"

"That's the frustrating thing," replied Pablo. "I can't even begin to describe it."

The guard then showed up and told Rose her visiting time was up. She neatly folded the letter and told Pedro she would be back tomorrow.

———

Pablo barely got to sleep when the next message came to his mind. He woke up and wrote it down.

*The second message—to Durango, Mexico*

"I know your affliction and your poverty, even though you are rich. I know the slander on the part of those who say that they are followers and are not, but are a synagogue of Satan. Do not fear what you are about to suffer. Beware, the devil is about to throw some of you into prison so that you may be tested, and for ten days you will have affliction. Be faithful until death, and I will give you the crown of life. Let anyone who has an ear listen to what the Spirit is saying to the churches. Whoever conquers will not be harmed by the second death." Pablo didn't know this church and he felt bad for them due to the challenging letter. Nonetheless, he wrote the following:

Your virtue is being faithful unto death.
Your vice is the fear of suffering.
My advice is to conquer the second death (going to Hell) through faith.

————

This time he decided to stay awake, and sure enough a strange vision developed. Rather than seeing anything, he heard music. Now Pablo enjoyed music, because in the midst of having his eyes rendered useless on the road to Tucson, he learned to listen carefully. In all, he heard five hymns. The first song celebrated the triune holiness of God. The second hymn gave honor to God as the creator, ending with "for you created all things, and by your will they existed and were created." The third piece of music reminded Pablo about the teachings he received from Jim Caldwell, because it talked about the opening of seals. Every Caldwellian knew the story about Kate at the diamond mine, and how six seals were broken when she arrived. As she reached toward the seventh seal, it too broke and the stone rolled away. The empty tomb proved not to have given up the body of Jim to grave robbers, because the risen Lord appeared many times to many people.

Rose could hardly wait to get in to see Pablo, and they discussed the meanings to no avail. Pablo seemed irritated, so he just handed her the next letter.

"Jim spoke to you again?" she asked.

"At least his letters," complained Pablo, "are easier to understand than these vision things."

The guard opened the door and told Rose it was time to go.

———————

That night Pablo began to wonder what was going on. It was easily the middle of the night, and nothing had yet happened. Just as Pablo was drifting off, he was woken up for the nightly message.

*The third message—to Cheyenne, Wyoming*

"I know where you are living, where Satan's throne is. Yet you are holding fast to my name, and you did not deny your faith in me even in the days of martyrdom. But I have a few things against you: you have some there who hold to the teachings of gambling and practice fornication. So you also have some who hold to the teaching of the one who was martyred. Repent then. If not, I will come to you soon and make war against them with the sword of my mouth. Let anyone who has an ear listen to what the Spirit is saying to the churches. To everyone who conquers I will give some of the hidden manna, and I will give a white stone, and on the white stone is written a new name that no one knows except the one who receives it."

This time Pablo decided to argue with Jim. "Are you sure you want to start with, 'I know where you are living'? Doesn't that sound a bit threatening?" Pablo got no answer, but he felt strangely humiliated. Sort of felt like he needed to stay in his own lane. Pablo soon realized his ego was messing with him, so he at least got to write his opinions to the church:

> Your virtue is that you did not deny Jim.
> Your vice is spiritual compromise.
> My advice is to repent or fall apart.

————

When he was done writing the letter, he started to remember the rest of the music vision he had the night before. When Rose arrived that morning, he excitedly shared that, "the fourth bit of singing entailed thousands upon thousands singing with full voice about Jim Caldwell. I think the hymn they they were singing was, 'O for a Thousand Tongues to Sing.'"

Rose asked, "What are you talking about?"

"Sorry," he said, "It's the rest of that music vision I started to tell you about."

"Okay, but slow down," suggested Rose.

Pablo realized that the fourth hymn was about seven honors being bestowed upon Jim, of "power and wealth and wisdom and might and honor and glory and blessing."

The guard started to approach, and Rose said, "This is ridiculous. I make a treacherous water crossing every day to get here, so I want more time." The guard acknowledged the situation and walked away.

Rose then looked at Pablo and said, "Hmm, sounds like strange honors. He had God's power here on earth. He didn't care about wealth. He was the wisest man I ever knew, although I only heard him teach one time. Jim sure had might, just not in earthly terms. Honor was certainly given to him by his followers. Now what were the other two?" Pablo said, "glory and blessing." Rose kind of frowned and said, "Jim never wanted glory and he was certainly a blessing."

Pablo annoyingly said, "Thanks, Rose, not real helpful, but here's the fifth song. It was being sung by "every creature in heaven and on earth and under the earth and in the sea, and all that is in them." Pablo was a bit surprised when it said, "To the one seated on the throne and to the Lamb." That made it clear that Jim was equal to God. He knew that Jim had been presented as a human, so he was glad that in his letter to the Caldwellians of San Francisco he said that Jim "was declared to be Son of God with power according to the spirit of holiness by resurrection from the dead." That made Pablo smile because the song celebrated the fulfillment of that truth. Then Rose made her required departure after taking the third letter

———————

That night Pablo tried to barter with Jim. "I'd like to get a good night's sleep, so is there any chance you could tell me the next message now?" It wasn't as if Jim was complying so much as the timing was right, but the message came and Pablo wrote it down.

*The fourth message—to Wichita, Kansas*

"I know your works—your love, faith, service, and patient endurance. I know that your last works are greater than the first.

# The Value of the Diamond

But I have this against you: you tolerate that Jezebel, who calls herself a prophet and is teaching and beguiling my servants to practice fornication. I gave her time to repent, but she refuses to repent of her fornication. Beware, I am throwing her on a bed, and those who commit adultery with her I am throwing into great distress, unless they repent of her doings; and I will strike her children dead. And all the churches will know that I am the one who searches minds and hearts, and I will give to each of you as your works deserve. But to the rest of you in Wichita, who do not hold this teaching, who have not learned what some call 'the deep things of Satan,' to you I say, I do not lay on you any other burden; only hold fast to what you have. To the one who conquers I will also give the morning star. Let anyone who has an ear listen to what the Spirit is saying to the churches." Then Pablo offered his summary thoughts:

Your virtue is growing in faith.
Your vice is moral compromise.
My advice is to hold fast to your faith.

——

When Rose arrived, she asked, "Did you have another vision?"

He told her that a very lengthy account was shared, that when it was done, he was able to understand it was about the struggle of the church in the midst of conflict and persecution. Pablo knew a thing or two about conflict and persecution, and Rose knew it, too. He told her that the even bigger story was about the judgments of God upon the enemies of the church.

# The Value of the Diamond

Pablo said, "The vision started symbolically with the seven seals on Jim's tomb being opened by Jim himself. The first seal opened, and a white steed came forth meaning conquest. The second seal opened and a red stallion emerged representing war. The third seal opened and a black horse appeared signifying famine. Then the fourth seal opened, and a pale green mare was there, and its rider's name was death."

"What did it mean?" Rose asked rather anxiously.

"That's what I asked Jim", then Pablo said, "and Jim told me that the white horse rider has a bow, signifying that the enemies of God will have some victories."

"I don't like that one," Rose said cautiously.

Then Pablo continued, "The red horse rider has a sword, signifying that war and bloodshed comes when people oppose God's rule."

"Not any better," said Rose, "but understandable."

Pablo continued, "The black horse rider is carrying scales, signifying the injustice of famine that follows war.

"Still making sense," said Rose.

Then Pablo said, "The pale green horse rider signifies hell and death, which naturally follow."

"Naturally," said Rose, "but what should we do?"

Pablo told her, "That's what I asked Jim, and he replied, "Love one another. God loves people enough to give them free will. Freely choose good."

Of course, the guard showed up at that point and sent Rose on her way. She took the fourth letter, and as she walked through the door she said, "Can't wait to hear about the opening of the last three seals."

---

# The Value of the Diamond

That night Pablo suggested to Jim, "Why not mix it up a little and give me the vision before the letter?" As expected, he was ignored. Being very tired, he quickly drifted off to sleep. For a while. Then the message came, waking him up, and he wrote it down.

*The fifth message—to Oklahoma City, Oklahoma*

"I know your works; you have a name of being alive, but you are dead. Wake up, and strengthen what remains and is on the point of death, for I have not found your works perfect in the sight of my God. Remember then what you received and heard; obey it, and repent. If you do not wake up, I will come like a thief, and you will not know at what hour I will come to you. Yet you have still a few persons who have not soiled their clothes; they will walk with me, dressed in white, for they are worthy. If you conquer, you will be clothed like them in white robes, and I will not blot your name out of the book of life; I will confess your name before my Father and before his angels. Let anyone who has an ear listen to what the Spirit is saying to the churches." Then Pablo wrote the following:

Your virtue is that you have lively works.
    That makes me, Pablo, very happy.
Your vice is that you are spiritually dead.
    That makes me, Pablo again, very sad.
My advice is to wake up your faith.

———

# The Value of the Diamond

"Okay," said Rose, "continue."

Pablo barely realized he'd been moved to the visitation room, so he took a moment to clear his head.

"Wow," said Pablo, "I don't know if I was in heaven again last night or not. At least the vision took place in heaven. The fifth seal was opened by Jim, and the martyrs were pleading for vindication, and were told to 'rest a little longer.'"

"Seems tiresome," announced Rose.

Pablo smiled and agreed, then said, "Jim opened the sixth seal, granting a view of God's punishments of the wicked."

"Wouldn't it be better," asked Rose, "to simply be good people?"

Pablo responded, "I think that's the point of the vision."

"What about the seventh seal?" asked Rose.

Pablo said, "It didn't happen next. First there was an interlude of two visions of assurance that God's people are secure from the plagues and judgments."

"That sounds better," Rose said with a smile.

Pablo continued, "Then Jim Caldwell opened the seventh seal, and as the legend goes, 'there was silence in heaven for about half an hour.'"

"That sounds good," commented Rose, but Pablo said "It turned out this calm was like the eye of the hurricane. Pablo wasn't sure he was ready for more of the vision, but it came right then and there.

"You look sick, Pablo," said Rose with a very concerned voice.

He said, "Quiet. Here's more." His eyes rolled upward and he said, "There's a sequence of six trumpets, followed by another interlude and then the seventh trumpet." Pablo thought that ended it, but loud voices in heaven said,

# The Value of the Diamond

"The nations raged,
  but your wrath has come,
  and the time for judging the dead,
for rewarding your servants, the prophets
  and saints and all who fear your name,
  both small and great,
and for destroying those who destroy the earth."

The guard heard all of this and didn't like it. He grabbed Rose's arm and said "It's time to go." Pablo had broken into a sweat, but Rose asked the guard if she could at least get the letter she was supposed to have from Pablo. It was visible in a pocket, so the guard grabbed it, gave it to her, and they left. At the front door, Rose asked if Pablo could get some medical help, but all he said was, "This island brings on all kinds of illnesses."

---

Pablo didn't seem to be doing much better that night, but he was startled awake by the next message. Not having much energy, Pablo went ahead and dutifully wrote it down.

*The sixth message—to San Antonio, Texas*

"I know your works. Look, I have set before you an open door, which no one is able to shut. I know that you have but little power, and yet you have kept my word and have not denied my name. I will make those of the synagogue of Satan who say that they are Jews and are not, but are lying—I will make them come and bow down before your feet, and they will learn that I have loved you. Because you have kept my word of patient endurance, I will keep you from the hour of trial that is coming on the whole world to test the inhabitants of the earth. Hold fast to what you have, so that no one may seize your crown. If you conquer, I will make you a pillar in the temple of my God; you will never go out of it. I will write on you the name of my God, and the name of the city of my God, the New Jerusalem that comes down from my God out of heaven, and my own new name. Let anyone who has an ear listen to what the Spirit is saying to the churches." Then Pablo added:

Your virtue is that you kept God's word.
Your vice is that you lack evangelism.
My advice is to keep the faith.

———

Desperately wanting to get back to sleep. The next vision came. It was a parable about evil, followed by yet another interlude, this one being three visions of reassurance. Then there was a sequence of the seven bowls of wrath. Pablo interrupted and asked Jim Caldwell if this was really necessary, to which Jim replied that God rules, so the readers of these visions are not to get discouraged or lose faith. The vision continued about the last days of the evil city. Pablo asked which evil city Jim was talking about, and he said, "Remember the messages to the seven churches?" Pablo said, "Yes." Jim said, "They represented all churches, and the evil city represents evil in every city."

# The Value of the Diamond

The next day he was looking forward to his visit from Rose, but it never came. He stopped a guard and asked if there was a problem with visitations, and the guard told him that the wind was fierce outside. Boats weren't able to make the dangerous passage across the frigid, shark-infested water.

---

It was a long day for Pablo. He still wasn't feeling very well, and he couldn't seem to get any medical attention. In his frustration, he thought about trying to escape. Nighttime mercifully came, along with another message, which he carefully wrote down.

*The seventh message—to Oaxaca, Mexico*

"I know your works; you are neither cold nor hot. I wish that you were either cold or hot. So, because you are lukewarm, and neither cold nor hot, I am about to spit you out of my mouth. For you say, 'I am rich, I have prospered, and I need nothing.' You do not realize that you are wretched, pitiable, poor, blind, and naked. Therefore I counsel you to buy from me gold refined by fire so that you may be rich; and white robes to clothe you and to keep the shame of your nakedness from being seen; and salve to anoint your eyes so that you may see. I reprove and discipline those whom I love. Be earnest, therefore, and repent. Listen! I am standing at the door, I will come to you and eat with you, and you with me. To the one who conquers I will give a place with my throne, just as I myself conquered and sat down with my Father on his throne. Let anyone who has an ear listen to what the Spirit is saying to the churches." Then Pablo offered his final summary:

Your virtue is that you are not against God.
Your vice is that you are not for God.
My advice is to take a stand (in fear and trembling).

———

Rose made it back the next day and got both of the last two letters. Pablo was still looking a bit peaked, but he had a lot of vision to tell her about. The vision shifted to God's redemption, through seven visions, to give ideas of a bigger picture than we could fully imagine.

"Great," said Rose, "so tell me about them."

The first vision," Pablo shared, "was the return of Jim whose name is called 'The Word of God.'

Rose had a lot of questions about that one. She realized this would take longer than usual, so she called the guard over and offered him some money for extra time. He gladly took the money and said, "Take all the time you need." Rose then looked back to Pablo and asked, "So does that mean Jim is the Bible?"

Pablo said, "Great question! And no, not particularly. We are all the Word of God when we act accordingly."

"And that's our task," said a smiling Rose.

"The second vision was the last battle," expounded Pablo.

Rose thought that sounded ominous, but Pablo explained that it was really more about God's victory.

"The third vision," shared Pablo, "was the binding of Satan, signifying that the reign of evil is not permanent."

"I love that!" offered Rose.

Pablo continued by saying, "The fourth vision was about the millennium, which is only for the martyrs. The point being that this earth would finally get to enjoy the Garden of Eden as intended."

"This stuff gets better all the time!" exclaimed Rose.

Pablo said, "The fifth vision was about the ultimate destruction of evil."

"Wow!" shouted Rose, at which time the guard told her to keep it quiet.

The two of them sat for a minute, the Pablo said, "The sixth vision was about the last judgment, depicted by two books. One represented human responsibility, so that people are judged by what they have done. The other is the book of life, in which people are saved not by what they have done but by what God has done."

Rose thought out loud, "Seems fair."

Pablo then told Rose about the seventh vision. "It was about the New Jerusalem, where redemption is not about making "all new things" but "all things new.""

He then leaned across the table a little closer to Rose and said, "I asked Jim if we can make heaven on earth by living your kingdom here and now? And you know what he said?"

Rose could barely wait for an answer. "Jim didn't say anything," Pablo said, "but he appeared to me, and smiled and winked."

At that point Jim whispered something to Rose, and she got up and left.

---

# The Value of the Diamond

That night Angel Island seemed to fulfil its name, because Pablo shockingly escaped. Nobody had ever escaped the island before, because it was far too treacherous of a crossing to swim, particularly at night. Not a lot of effort was put into finding Pablo because he wasn't deemed a threat. His body also never washed ashore and likewise, he was never found. Soon enough, people in the area forgot about Pablo, but intriguingly, word got around that his letters started arriving little by little to the seven churches. Each time, they were delivered by a man and a woman on horseback, who disappeared as quickly as they arrived.

## WATCH FOR THE START OF:

# THE KING MONTEZUMA TRILOGY

*The Forming of the Empire: A King Montezuma Story: Book 1* is set during The Formative and Classic Period of Mesoamerica. It begins in the jungles of Guatemala and ends in Mexico. It retells the stories of the biblical Law, through the time of the judges. It will be published in the spring of 2024.

*The Secret of the Empire: A King Montezuma Story: Book 2* deals with the development of kings through the prophecies of shamans. The Aztec Empire ended on August 13, 1521 when Herman Cortes and the Spanish Conquistadors overthrew King Montezuma. It retells the stories of the biblical Prophets, setting them in the Postclassic Period of Mesoamerica. It will be published in the fall of 2024.

*The Value of the Empire: A King Montezuma Story: Book 3* tells the stories left behind, of legends, wisdom, art, and poetry. It retells the stories of the biblical Writings, set in what is now Mexico City. It will be published in the spring of 2025. It also paves the way for The Jim Caldwell Trilogy.

# ACKNOWLEDGMENTS

The *New Revised Standard Version* (NRSV) of *The Holy Bible* is used when scriptures are referenced.

Thanks goes to Dave Raines for volunteering to be my beta reader. His friendship for over forty years has been immensely appreciated, as I wandered through the wilderness of ministry. I truly believe the promised land is ahead.

Thanks goes to my amazing wife, the Rev. Dr. Yvonne C. Oropeza, for being my development editor. Her love, support, and talent have made an immense impact on this book.

FYI. The Prologue covers the resurrection. Scene One in all four Acts of this book, deals with the Book of Acts. Scene Two in all four Acts, deals with letters of Paul, and the Epilogue covers the Book of Revelation.

# BOOKS BY THIS AUTHOR

## NONFICTION

### A Serious In-Depth Bible Study Trilogy

**A Natural History of Scripture: How the Bible Evolved— Book 1.**

A deconstruction of biblical formation as seen through the lens of evolutionary biology.

**Wrestling with Scripture: How to Interpret the Bible— Book 2.**

How to interpret the Bible's original Greek and Hebrew by using word study tools.

**Practicing Scripture: How to Live the Bible—Book 3.**

How to put the ideas from the Bible into every day practice.

**How to Lead a Celebration of Life**

# The Value of the Diamond

An indispensable guide for laity and clergy to conduct a funeral with meaning and integrity.

## Don't Look a Camel in the Mouth: Pilgrimages through the Land of Jesus and Paul

The author shares five pilgrimages through the Holy Land, Turkey, Greece, Italy, and the Mediterranean.

## Don't Look a Camel in the Mouth: A Spiritual Journal Companion Book

This book follows *Don't Look a Camel in the Mouth: Pilgrimages through the Land of Jesus and Paul* with meditation questions for spiritual growth.

## Parish the Thought: An Eye-Opening Look Behind the Pulpit

The author and his wife share stories of their 37 years in the ministry.

## Austria, Germany, and the Oberammergau Passion Play

The author shares his experiences leading a group to this famous play, and the surrounding area.

# The Value of the Diamond

**Your Year of Spiritual Growth: A Biblical Journey**

This book creates spirituality through daily scripture readings, devotional questions, and debriefing with others.

# FICTION

## A Jim Caldwell Trilogy

**The Forming of the Diamond: A Jim Caldwell Story: Book 1.**

This is a retelling of the life of Jesus, drawn from the four gospels, looking through the lens of the American Old West. It focuses on The Sermon on the Mount, and shares some of the parables and healings

**The Secret of the Diamond: A Jim Caldwell Story: Book 2.**

This is a creative retelling of the last days of Jesus, set in Phoenix in 1881. It is the middle book of the Jim Caldwell trilogy. It deals with the Passion Narrative, from Gethsemane to the grave, which I call the diamond of the Gospel.

**The Value of the Diamond: A Jim Caldwell Story: Book 3.**

# The Value of the Diamond

This current book deals with the resurrection, and tells the story of the early church from the Book of Acts and the Letters of Paul, ending with the Book of Revelation.

**The Secret of the Diamond: A Lenten Devotional.**

A Companion piece for *The Secret of the Diamond: A Jim Caldwell Story: Book 2.*

-----------

If you enjoy my books, please review them on Amazon, Goodreads, Barnes & Noble, or any of your favorite places.

# The Value of the Diamond

www.ingramcontent.com/pod-product-compliance
Lightning Source LLC
Chambersburg PA
CBHW060206070426
42447CB00035B/2736